FREEDOM

OF

SPEECH!

IN A SOCIETY THAT STINKS!

Barry J Steel

"Freedom is a myth"

Patrick McGoohan

BARRY J STEEL

AUTHOR OF

THAILAND AFTER DIVORCE

RIGS, PIGS AND DIRTY DIGS

FREEDOM OF SPEECH! IN A SOCIETY THAT STINKS!

Barry is on Facebook

(NOT the man who looks like he's being secretly fellated by a dog)

With thanks to Pete (Kojak),
for the J, for the advice,
for being my first customer
and first reviewer. You really
have been a good little lapdog.

Also a special thanks to
Brian Obama
Alysha Merkel
Titan Blair
And
Jihadi 'Boy Fingerer' John
For the generous quotes

In Memory Of

Jean Cabut
Elsa Cayat
Stephane Charbonnier
Philippe Honore
Bernard Marris
Mustupa Ourad
Bernard Verlhac
Georges Wolinski

CONTENTS

INTRODUCTION

Dear reader, welcome back and once again many thanks for purchasing one of my books. I really can't believe that you're still handing your money over to me!

They say it takes time for an author to find their own writing style. Now first of all I should point out that I still don't consider myself to be an author but the last statement does ring true. My first two books are *very* different from one another. With my debut I had tried my hardest to sound like a genuine author and my second book was just me being me. This instalment is an amalgamation of the first two and it's possibly the best that my *very* limited writing capability will allow.

Apparently when an author of fiction starts writing a new book they will always have a beginning and an end. When they do the hard part of writing the middle they find that the ending is nothing like the one originally intended. When I started writing this book, in early December 2014, I didn't have a clue what the upcoming period of my life was going to be like. I had hoped life would carry on as it had been, with continuous work offshore. Unfortunately for me that wasn't to be the case…fortunate for you however because that book would have been even duller than the one you're holding in your hands right now.

I had finished my previous book saying it would take me a couple of years to write this one. When I wrote those words last September I believed them to be true, but the unforeseen events that lay in front of me set this book off in a totally different direction and I've been able to complete it in less than half that time.

The first working title for this was 'Life After Thailand' and it was going to have a plain cover like my debut. Then, in a nod to the first line of my second book, the title was changed to 'I Feel Like Weeping' and the cover was going to be a photo of a snotty bellend. I realised that cover would probably destroy the books sales. I had the idea for a huge childish cock drawn onto the side of a cooling tower at around the same time as a very horrific news report was showing on the telly and a new title was born.

This is a direct follow up to my debut and I'm taking it for granted that you've read my first book. If you haven't there will be a couple of lines in the first two chapters that won't make much sense to you, but don't worry, you shouldn't find them to be too distracting. If you are brand new to one of my books then you need to know that it is not my intention to shock…merely deliver to you the harsh brutal truth!

WARNING- If a person were to step into a male dominated, working class environment they would discover that we men still use words that have been deemed outdated and politically incorrect by the rest of society. To give you an authentic view of life in my industry these words have been retained in this book and I can assure you that no offence is intended in their use. This is just how we fucking speak!

"As I walk down the high street I see a sight that stops me in my tracks and makes me want to vomit all over my own shoes! It's a big fat Arab woman dressed in sheets and she's gliding along on a mobility scooter. As she glides past I shake my head in disgust and think to myself, *'That one woman symbolises everything that is wrong in this shit society!'* "

CHAPTER ONE

THE IMMEDIATE AFTERMATH

It's July 2014 and I'm sat on a hotel balcony in Pattaya, Thailand. I'm feeling like shit after having a fever two nights earlier. Laid on my bed in the hotel room is a woman who hates me. A thought crosses my mind, *'I wish I was back at home in England'.* In the four holidays that I'd had in Pattaya, this was the first time that I'd ever had this thought. When I did return home I'd felt bored and disillusioned with that city, I needed to go somewhere else in the world. I told myself to give it at least another year before returning…

A couple of months after that last holiday I had a very memorable week. Due to cutbacks at work I lost the longest and best job I'd ever had, I released my first book and very quickly realised it wasn't going to sell and worst of all my kids told me that they didn't want to sleep at my house. It was a bad week dear reader, but it wasn't completely unexpected.

I had just had the best year of my entire life so far, you can't expect to ride on a peak for that long without eventually crashing straight into a trough. For the majority of that year I had been 32 years old and it's an age that I will never forget. During this bad stage I filled my time by drinking whisky on the night and during the day I was helping my mate to build his shed on his new allotment.

I had never been on an allotment before and I quickly grew to realise that the people who own them are very strange and very annoying. These people are friendly and helpful but they are also extremely nosey and some of them carry an air of unfounded superiority (the pigeon keepers especially had a plastic gangster whiff about them). My friend and I were building this shed from scratch, something neither of us had ever done before. The majority of the wood we used was gifted to us from these friendly, nosey people. The pessimist in me suspected that they had a hidden agenda of getting my friend firmly in their pockets! When we stood back and looked with pride at the finished exterior, my friend and I saw a work of art...everybody else just saw a shed.

I can hear you asking, *'Why is he waffling on about a shed?'* You need to know that shed helped me get through a couple of horrific weeks of my life. It occupied my mind during the daytime. When my mind wasn't occupied by that shed it was occupied by a place…Pattaya! Only two months earlier I thought I'd grown tired of that city, now it was all I could think about. But I thought about it in a way that was completely different to how I had ever thought about it in the past. I'd wanted to return there after each holiday because I loved the place but now I wanted to go there to escape. I have never ran from a problem in my life, I have always 'faced the music'. That is the best way to be in life, but here I was now, desperate to run away from everything.

When my debut book was released my naïve plans for advertising it quickly unfolded. Due to my complete lack of knowledge of social media I thought that I would just be able to join some Thailand forums and advertise my book on them. It wasn't that simple. All my posts were immediately deleted and one forum sent me a message saying that I was breaching advertising rules and my account had been suspended! I had written a book that nobody knew existed.

I've mentioned in my previous books of my own laziness and after this set back I decided to just leave it. Other than a few posts on an offshore forum and a dreadful YouTube video, I made no more attempts to advertise the book. By now however I had already finished my second book, in a shrewd business move I changed the title of the book to appeal to offshore workers and contractors, whom I knew I could advertise it to for free. I didn't want to rush into releasing that book straight away though, I decided to sit on it for a few months. The failure of my book sales and the loss of a job were the least of my worries that week though.

Dear reader, there's something about my divorce that I didn't tell you about in my first book. Two weeks after I left my wife I phoned her up and offered to,
    "Come back home for the sake of the kids."
I had been wracked with guilt since leaving them. The next day she gave me her reply,
    "No"
 The majority of my guilt left me in an instant and I felt free to get on with my life. (I was to find out from her father later on down the line that she hadn't been happy with the wording of my proposal) As the months rolled by she realised that I had absolutely no intention of ever trying to get back with her and she also found out I had booked a holiday to Thailand. She began to use the kids against me. Although I always had plenty of time with them she completely took away any say that I had in their lives. Just after Christmas 2012 things between us erupted and I was pushed to breaking point. Luckily a week later I was enjoying my first ever trip to Pattaya and when I got there I completely forgot about England and all the

problems that I had. When I returned home all those problems came rushing back and I was forced to make a choice...carry on stressing out until I ended up in a loony bin or I could build, what the band Pink Floyd would describe as, a wall. I chose the latter option. But building a wall brings its own list of problems.

In October 2014 my kids told me that they would rather stop with *'mammy's boyfriend'* than me...it wasn't a very pleasant moment in my life. This incident happened after months of arguing with the ex, and this bout of arguments had started whilst I was sat in the airport waiting to go to Pattaya for the fourth time. The following week things became even worse when my family mistook my way of dealing with things as 'indifference'...they got pissed off with me.

At this bad time I was offered one week's work offshore and on the train up to Aberdeen I planned my escape. A little bit of common sense in me was screaming out not to go back to Thailand. After this job I knew I would be unemployed at the worst possible time of year for a man with my trade and I didn't have much money in the bank. I also knew that if I did this now then running away to Pattaya every time I have a problem *could* become something that I will do for the rest of my life. But that common sense only had a small voice and the much louder voice was screaming, *'Get the fuck out of this shit country as soon as possible!'*

During that one week offshore I looked at hotel and flight prices. I emailed my last hotel and they gave me a good offer on a room, I took it and booked twenty-four nights. I had to resist the urge to book the full twenty-nine nights that my visa would allow. Resisting that urge however, would end up costing me a *lot* of money.

Even though I had a holiday to look forward to now, Mr Bad Luck let me know he hadn't forgotten about me by giving me another kick in the bollocks. My train journey home from that trip offshore ended up taking double the normal time. When I was finally stood on my doorstep at 23:00 I realised I had completely lost my house key. All other copies of it were in my house so I had no option but to phone an emergency locksmith. Forty minutes later a man turned up, he showed me just how easy it was to break into my house and then charged me £115 for the privilege. Bastard!

Three days later I was sat in the airport feeling very excited. In fact it was the most excited that I had ever felt of all the times that I'd sat there. I had drawn comparisons to my very first and best holiday to Pattaya…like then I was going away at a time when I was unemployed and had horrendous problems at home. I also knew that after the complete disaster that had been my last holiday, this one could only be better. I had a feeling it was going to be good, I just could never have imagined how good it actually turned out to be.

Of course there was one little problem though. I knew about the Pattaya Blues and due to what I would be returning home to, I knew that I was going to be suffering from a horrific bout of it in the very near future. Dear reader I did what I do best, I completely blocked that thought from my mind.

CHAPTER TWO

REKINDLING A LOST PASSION

1

On the 30th October 2014 I set off on my fifth holiday to Thailand. The flight from Newcastle to Dubai was the most enjoyable flight that I've ever had. This was due to the company of an old bloke from Scotland. Together we sat and drank Scotch on ice and had a good chinwag, he was a very nice man. Sat in front of us was a young Englishman and his Thai girlfriend. She was an absolute embarrassment! She was young and pretty but she was drunk and behaving in a way that I wouldn't let my young daughter get away with. At one point she was even rude to a very patient air hostess!

The young man overheard me saying that I worked offshore and he turned around and started talking to me. It turned out that he was an offshore diver. Surprisingly for a diver he wasn't an arrogant wanker, he was actually quite nice.

Once we were in Dubai airport we got to know each other a bit better, he was 25 and he was also going to Pattaya. He didn't own a house in England, he lived in £125,000 condo in Thailand. For that price it must be a luxurious pad. In this short time together my distaste for his girlfriend grew even more. She was wearing a skimpy dress so it was impossible to miss the large tattoo on her thigh. When I saw that tattoo I knew immediately that he will have met her in a gogo bar and then when he told me that he absolutely hated Walking Street (the main place in Pattaya) it confirmed my suspicions. I'm guessing that street is where he met her and it's a constant reminder to him of her old 'profession'.

I noticed that he did everything for this spoilt little brat, he was what we call in England an absolute 'carpet'! We talked about sharing a taxi once we got to Bangkok and he told me a story which annoyed me somewhat.

"The last time she made this journey she was on her own and when she got to Bangkok she jumped straight into a limo. It cost 7000 baht"

Dear reader, a taxi from Bangkok to Pattaya is an absolute maximum of 1500 baht. I've said in the past that I'm a straight talking man and my immediate response was,

"If it were me I would've got rid of her"

He gave an awkward laugh and said,

"She was just tired from a long journey. It's understandable really"
I really couldn't believe what I was listening to! There was one point we were travelling up an escalator and he was stood facing me, she grabbed his crotch in front of everyone there, he looked really embarrassed and I felt embarrassed for him. He then told me that they were going to start trying for a baby! When he said this I felt like grabbing him and shaking some sense into him. He was young, good looking, had a good job and he was about to destroy his life with that creature! I never did bump into them in Bangkok airport so I ended up getting a taxi on my own. It was a relief really, although he was a really nice lad his patheticism was grinding on me.

My taxi ran into a storm halfway into the journey to Pattaya. I had been in every season by now and I'd always been lucky with the weather. Even in the rainy season I'd barely seen any rain. I had heard that Pattaya was prone to flooding, when I got there I saw it with my own eyes for the first time. Beach Road was so deep in water that you couldn't see the footpath or beach that ran alongside it. I didn't let it bother me, I was just excited to be back there. In fact when I did get there I felt like I was where I belong, all worries and stress completely vanished. I was greeted by all the hotel staff who already knew me and then I unpacked and went straight to a bar where I was immediately thrown into conversation with a beautiful Thai woman.

I've never really suffered from bad jetlag on my trips to Thailand, each first night is normally a drunken blur but the next night I'll be straight into it. This time I had barely slept on the plane and for the first two nights I felt absolutely fucked. I have always had a first night tradition of going to Walking Street but on this fifth holiday the tradition was lost and I didn't leave Soi 8. It would be the second night that I ventured to that infamous road but when I got there I was delivered some devastating news...Xzone, my favourite gogo bar had closed down! I was crushed dear reader, I felt like dropping to my knees in the middle of the street, throwing my hands to the sky and screaming NO!...but instead of doing that I just turned around and went to a different bar.

I had gone on this trip with one goal in mind and that was to be a sex animal! I started off well. When I awoke on my fifth day I'd already been with seven women. When I say women I must confess that one of them was actually a drop dead gorgeous ladyboy. After my night with her I told myself that I wouldn't have any more ladyboy's this holiday. It appeared that hanging out the back of a bloke had lost its original charm.

There was one thing that I'd had no intention of doing this trip though and that was meeting Ann again. Contact with her had stopped after the last holiday and so far I'd completely avoided her bar. However there was one problem that I knew I couldn't contend with and that was the fact that she had friends everywhere! On day six I turned on my phone to check my messages and a message came through from Ann,

'Are you in Pattaya now? I hope you have a nice holiday'

I gave a simple reply,

'Yes'

Immediately another message came through,

'How long have you been here?'

'6 days'

'Good for you. Where you stay?'

I'll cut a long story short dear reader, I caved in and she ended up coming to my room. When she arrived she pretended to be pissed off with me but I could see that really, she was just happy to see me again. I'll be honest, it was nice to see her again and I needed a bit of a rest. I was feeling rough so she went out and got me my favourite Thai food. That night I took her to my favourite bar and whilst we were sat there I had the misfortune of seeing the ugliest, fattest greasy bastard that I had seen so far in that city. He had a face that looked like it was felching a yeti!

In Pattaya you see all sorts of men, midgets, people with limbs missing, heavily disabled men, even banana packers! Whenever I see these men I think, *'Good for you'*, it's not their fault that they're the way that they are. However I'll never get used to the sight of these big greasy obese men. They have nobody to blame but themselves and they always seem to have the worst attitude towards the girls. At home I imagine that they have jobs in management and are used to bullying people around. They make me feel sick!

2

There was a night on this holiday that I had really been looking forward to, the Loi Krathong festival, which celebrates the end of the rainy season. I had been there the previous year but unfortunately I hadn't been able to enjoy it properly due to the fact that it was the last night of my holiday and I had an early taxi ride the next morning.

When the festival came I took Ann to the beach and we sat together to soak in the sights. It's with great disappointment dear reader, that I have to confess that I didn't get to enjoy it this time either. The fact that Ann was sat in a sulk for some reason was the least of my worries. It was the sight of all the happy children on the beach. I'm good at blocking things out but this night I couldn't help thinking about my own kids and the mess I had left behind me in England. After an hour I gave up trying to enjoy it. It was still an impressive sight but like the previous year I really wasn't in the mood. I got up and left Ann sitting there in her sulk.

The next day I was laid on my bed telling Ann the story of the young Englishman and his horrible little Thai girlfriend on the plane. I can remember saying to her,

"I doubt she even loved him".

Ann told me that if he was young, handsome and had money then that is what all Thai women dream about so she *will* love him. My first question was,

"What if a man is old and rich?"

"Then the woman will not really love him."

"OK, so if she loves him because he is young, handsome and rich then that's not real love is it?"

"That doesn't matter."

Was her reply.

At one point she popped out to get us some food, so I decided to have a wank whilst she was gone. I can hear you murmuring, *'Wanking in Thailand?'* I understand your sentiment dear reader but trust me, every now and again you just need the real thing. I don't know the reason why but for the third holiday in a row now I had started cumming like a teenager. My muck would shoot right across my chest and onto the pillow behind me. Each time this happens it only lasts a few weeks before returning to the usual unimpressive dribble. As I sit here writing these words, picturing myself laid on that bed I have made an awful discovery! There is nothing more heart wrenching than the sight of a man, laid on his own in a Pattaya hotel room…masturbating!

In my first three holidays to Pattaya I had absolutely loved going to the beach, going there nearly every day. On my fourth holiday I had grown bored of the place and only went twice. On this fifth holiday I only went three times. The first time I was with Ann, we were sat there and I was doing my best to make her laugh. She had told me earlier that day that I moan too much! After half hour or so three Indians came and sat on the seats next to us. They sat there for forty minutes and for the entire time they never stopped eating! Whereas it's normally food sellers hounding the people sat down, this time it was these Indians hounding the food sellers.

The food on Pattaya beach is really cheap and I know that any Indian who can afford a holiday in Thailand isn't going to be short of cash. These three mingebag's were haggling down the sellers so much that a few of them just got pissed off and walked away from them. Me and Ann kept giving each other glances during these shenanigans. After they left I told Ann a story about something I saw on my very first holiday in Pattaya…

I had been sat on the beach on my own and five or six Indian men had come and sat on the chairs in front of me. To hire a chair and table for a full day costs 50 baht, which was roughly £1 at the time. The man who rented out the chairs approached the group of men and started talking to one of them.

"That's 50 baht please"

"50 baht for all of us?"

"No, 50 baht each"

"Each!! For one week?"

"No for one day"

"One day!!"

The Indian man then made a hand gesture to say 'no chance', the group all got up and then stormed away in a huff! What a bunch of fucking mingebag's!

Altogether I had six nights with Ann, apart from a minor spat on the Loi Krathong festival we had got on well. When I told her that I wanted a few nights on my own she wasn't having any of it. She told me that if she left again this time, then she was never coming back. To be honest I didn't believe her but when she stormed out of my room with all her gear it turned out to be the last I saw of her. I don't mind admitting that it would've been nice to see her again that holiday but I wasn't going to let it bother me. I hadn't gone there to fulfil her fairy-tale fantasy, I had gone there to be a dirty bastard and that's exactly what I was!

On Wednesday 12th November 2014 at the age of 33 I finally fulfilled my life's ambition...I had a squirter. It wasn't the big arterial spray that you see in porn films, it was more of a gentle gush. Maybe there are different levels of squirter's in the world but I was more than happy with the one I had. There were two things I noticed about this girl. Firstly, how easy it was to arouse her, simply rubbing the inside of her thigh made her quim shiver like a wet dog on a cold winter's day. Secondly, how easy it was to make her cum! I'm no Casanova in the bedroom but four times is something any man should be proud of and I'll admit to you now dear reader, I'm usually lucky if I can make a girl cum even once!

The first time it happened she was riding me as if someone was holding a gun to her head. After a time she just collapsed on top of me and that's when I felt it...warm liquid trickling down my balls and arse crack. The third time was the best! That night I found an energy that I didn't know existed in me. I was doing her from behind when all of a sudden she lurched forward off me and onto her belly. I then noticed that about eight square inches of the bed sheet was damp! They say when a man finally achieves his ultimate goal in life he has a period of depression soon after. I can assure you now, that no such depression fell upon me.

The night after the squirter I had the misfortune of venturing into my very first Russian gogo bar. It was on Walking Street and it's probably the most famous of them all. A word of advice, unless you're fucking loaded steer well clear of these places. I've always avoided them myself in the past but for some reason this night I just decided to take a peak. I sat down and ordered a whisky, it cost me £5 and I had to pay upfront! A Russian girl came and sat next to me and to my surprise she was actually a pleasant person. However during our chat three separate Russian girls came over and asked me if I would like them to dance for me. Each time I gave them the same answer and each time I got the same reply.

"I'm talking to her"

"So, I can still dance for you"

I'm confident that a woman of any other nationality wouldn't even consider approaching a man who was already sat with a woman.

I've said it before and I'll say it again Russians are fucking rude! They are brought up to have absolutely no basic manners whatsoever! (A bit like half the scaffolders I've ever met). Unfortunately on two separate occasions this holiday I couldn't bite my tongue any longer. I don't want to sound like a knob so I won't go into any details but let's just say I spat my dummy out with two different groups of Russians. In both of my previous books I have made comments about English tourists, I stand by those comments but I need to make an amendment…Russians are *the* worst tourists in the world! Even a drunken English wanker still manages to retain some basic manners.

3

The first half of my holiday had started really well. My first week I was my usual 'one man band' shag anything that moves. When that started to get a bit repetitive Ann showed up. I enjoyed my time with her but towards the end I was starting to get a bit sick of the girlfriend experience. There were three nights after Ann left where my holiday was in danger of becoming boring like my fourth one had been, but then it was completely changed. The change came in the shape of a 51 year old bald man from Australia called Greg.

I had first met Greg the day after Ann left, in a shop near my hotel. When I had walked in he said hello to me and we had a couple of minutes of small talk. A few days later I was in my hotel pool and Greg showed up, it turned out that he was stopping in the same hotel as me. Sometimes in life you immediately click with people and Greg and I clicked. I'm going to pay the Australians the biggest compliment that they have ever had…all they are is English people with stupid accents. They use the same slang words as us, they have the same sense of humour as us and they even eat exactly the same food as us.

Me and Greg sat in that pool chatting for around five hours without one awkward silence. He was a very funny man and he had that little bit of eccentricity that I like in a person. I know that in that first afternoon together sex wasn't mentioned, we seemed to talk about everything but that one subject. I can remember at one point he said something that made me want to laugh in his face, but because I didn't really know him I just about managed to contain it. I was talking to him about tipping the cleaners and he came out with this line,

"I like to give the staff bags of peanuts."

It was my first inkling that Greg was a mingebag.

That night we went to Walking Street together and got completely smashed. I took him to a couple of gogo bars he'd never been to before and he had his first experience of inserting ice cubes into respectable girls. The next afternoon in the pool sex was the only topic of conversation! It turned out he was a bigger pervert than me! He told me that, just that morning he'd received a blowjob from a woman with hardly any teeth that he'd found on Beach Road. This only made me like him even more. The subject of ladyboy's popped up and I was the first to admit to having done it. I then found out that Greg was *very* partial to the ladyboy's and the things he did with them were a few levels of perversity above what I was willing to do with them.

In my first book I mocked my friend for shitting himself, on this same afternoon I very nearly suffered the same fate. (You will find that a mix of Thai food and Thai whisky can play war with our western guts) As Greg and I were chatting we were joined in the pool by two more Aussies. I immediately felt the urge to have a poo but I didn't want to look like the Pommy scared out of the pool by a gang of Kangaroo Fuckers, so I decided to hold onto it for a bit. After a while it was forgotten about. The group of us chatted for more than an hour but when the pair of Aussies left, the feeling came back with a vengeance! I told Greg I was off to empty my bowels, I got out of the pool and headed straight for my room. The moment I started walking I had to clench my arse cheeks tight, I picked up pace and I must have looked like a waddling penguin. When I got into my room I had to run to the toilet and as I turned to sit down, crouching and lowering my shorts at the same time, it just sprayed out of me. All over the seat and all over the floor on one side of the pot. I had no option but to sit down in my own filth until it was all out of me! I felt like an old man, it was horrible.

That night Greg and I went out again but this time we just stayed on Soi 8. For some reason some men look at me and instantly dislike me, I don't know why and I don't really care. Greg and I were playing pool at a bar and we were taking it in turns to put songs on using a laptop computer. Sat at the bar was some scrawny little European man who had a face that looked like it had been put through a mangle. He was with his Thai girlfriend. At one point I was stood at the laptop choosing a song and he spoke to me. I honestly didn't hear what he said so I said to him,
    "Sorry mate?"
He stared at me and said,
    "I'll pick the next song."
To which I replied,
    "No worries."
Whilst I was saying that I noticed him give the girl a smarmy look that suggested to me he thought I was thick. I ignored it dear reader and went back to my game of pool. A few minutes later this wretch of a man walked up to me and held out a bag of fried crickets, which must have belonged to his 'girlfriend'. He held them up to my face and all he said was,
    "No worries *man*."

Without thinking twice I took a fried cricket from the bag and threw it straight into my mouth. His lass instantly burst out laughing and his face dropped, he went and sat down looking rather sheepish. He had basically tried to embarrass me and it backfired. He wasn't to know that since my very first holiday, after seeing the fried crickets and scorpions, I'd always wondered what they tasted like. To be honest it was just like eating crisps, only it got a bit chewy towards the end and left my mouth as dry as a camel's tit. Some men are pure wankers, but I suppose I have to thank him for giving me the opportunity to finally try them. (The shameless cunt ended up offering to buy me a drink!)

For the last two days I had been listening to Greg tell me about his love for singing and dancing. This night I got to see both for the very first time. He wasn't a bad singer at all but his dancing took me off guard. It was horrific! Greg is one of those men who doesn't give a fuck what anybody else thinks about him. When he danced he made a complete tit of himself and at first I didn't know how to take it. I could see the faces of everyone around us looking at him as if he was a lunatic. Pretty soon though I saw the funny side and started laughing at him. After that, every time he danced at a bar people would see me laughing and they would start laughing as well. I nicknamed Greg 'The Trumpet Player' because of the way he puckered his lips whilst he danced. Earlier that day I had also nicknamed him 'The Mingebag', it was a word he was unfamiliar with but he instantly fell in love with it. He promised to introduce the term to Australia, by the time I finish writing this book I hope it will have spread like the wildfire that ravages that country each year.

That night we parted company and when I saw Greg in the pool the next afternoon he said to me straight away,

"I've had three separate ladyboy's in the last nine hours!"

The man is a bona fide pervert! We got chatting about our antics of the night before. I can remember talking to him and at one point a vacant look came across his face, he clearly wasn't listening to what I was saying to him. He then suddenly put his hands to either side of his face and blurted out,

"I've just had a flashback...I let a ladyboy cum on top of my head last night!"

I burst out laughing. I never asked Greg what was happening in the moments before that incident took place, I really didn't want to know. I'm sure that lots of people in the world wouldn't know how to take Greg. If any of you readers thinks he comes across as a dick then just blame my writing. The man is a living legend

4

There's a story I'm going to tell you dear reader and by the time it's finished you might despise me…it's a risk I'm willing to take.

Every once and a while a man will have a really filthy night in his life. These nights normally come out of the blue, brought about by a number of unforeseen circumstances. On this night three things in particular led to it becoming filthy. The first thing was all of Greg's dirty ladyboy stories swimming around in my head, the second thing was around one litre of Sangsom and the final thing was using a friends phone to check my emails in a drunken state. When I read an email from Ann telling me that she fucking hated me, the wheels to my filthy night were put into motion. I wanted to do some damage and a ladyboy was the only option for me. (If you don't already know, it's me who nails them, NOT the other way round!)

Every night I'd walked past a stunning ladyboy on Soi 8, she always seemed keen for me to go with her and unfortunately for her on this night her wish came true! When we got to my room this *girl* gave me the best blowjob that I've ever had in my life. She had a pierced tongue and she was rubbing the stud all over my bellend, staring straight into my eyes whilst she was doing it. Then she started spitting on it! Now trust me dear reader, it doesn't take much to be able to deep throat me but I've still found it to be quite a rarity. This creature started deep throating me very aggressively, when I watched her doing it I seized the moment and tested the waters. I put both my hands on the back of her head and held it down. To my delight she didn't resist! That's when I knew I was going to get the night that I wanted.

At one point I was reaming its arse from behind, I had wrapped its hair around my left hand and had its head pulled back to breaking point, I was using my right hand to spank the fuck out of its arse cheeks. When I eventually came it was in its mouth after a *very* aggressive skull fucking. It even swallowed it! When she left the room I laid there feeling like Max Hardcore! (Minus the pissing and fisting). After that night that ladyboy begged me for the same brutal treatment every time I walked past her! What a pervert!

There was actually another porn star moment earlier on in the holiday. I was shagging a black girl and I found that I just couldn't cum because of the amount of alcohol in me. She told me to lay on my back and to start wanking myself off...I did as I was told. Whilst I was going for it she started sucking my right foot, then my ankle and she worked her way right up the inside of my leg with her bright pink tongue, staring me straight in the eyes the whole time. When she got to my balls she started gobbling on them! Its magical little moments like that, that make the Pattaya experience what it is.

Now every man has his own 'sex face', I've never seen mine but I know that it can't look very pleasant! The only time it ever emerges is when I'm doing a girl from behind and I'm starting to run out of steam, so luckily the woman never gets to see it. Unfortunately for this black girl, whilst I was thrashing the end off it I could feel my sex face emerge with a vengeance! Although her face didn't react, I could see in her eyes that she wasn't very impressed by it. I must have looked like a chimpanzee holding onto a pneumatic digger!

When it came to my last day I was sat in the pool with Greg trying not to be too miserable. The truth is, I *was* miserable, very fucking miserable and as the sun got lower in the sky that old feeling of impending doom returned. It took one little sentence from my lips to completely change everything,

"I feel like changing my flight"

As soon as I said it the damage was done and I couldn't get the thought out of my head. I spent the next hour or so arguing with myself. In the end I felt like I only had one option. I started a mission to stop in Pattaya.

I hadn't booked my flight direct with the airline, instead I had used an online agency. When I *finally* got through to the right person I was hit with some horrible news...the cost of changing my flight was going to be a fortune! I'm not going to say exactly how much but let's just say it was a *lot* more than what I'd actually paid for the original flight! I thought about it, panicked a bit and then told the girl on the phone,

"OK just do it."

She said to me,

"Are you sure?"

To which I replied,

"No, but I'll worry about that later."

With less than ninety minutes spare before my taxi was due I was suddenly stopping in Pattaya an extra five nights. The cost of the flight, hotel and spending money nearly wiped out the last of what I had in the bank. But I didn't care, I didn't have to go back home and that's all that mattered.

Hindsight is a terrible thing. If only I had just cancelled my flight and booked a new one on my own maybe I could've saved a lot of money. I know now that every future holiday that I have in Thailand I'm going to have to use up the full length of my visa or almost certainly I will just end up in that same situation again. To make up for my stupid, and to be honest, pathetic behaviour I made that last week the best week of the holiday by far.

5

The first night of my extended stay Greg and I went out and got absolutely trolleyed. Greg kept me entertained all night with his singing and 'dancing' and the feeling of pain that I'd had from the cost of changing my flight slowly disappeared. As we drank into the wee hours it was time to find some ladies. Due to Greg's mingebagism he would occasionally get girls from Beach Road to save some money. I myself, generally avoid these women but this night I decided to follow him. Almost immediately a lady caught my eye, we had a brief chat and she seemed really nice. Soon after we were sat on my balcony drinking and chatting. To my surprise she was 37 years old, she looked 10 years younger than that. She was funny and she was good company.

When it came to the doing the business she turned out to be possibly the best shag that I've ever had in my life! Some of the manoeuvres she pulled off were absolutely amazing. Though she didn't stand a chance of beating the blowjob that I'd had off that ladyboy, she made up for it by laying legs akimbo and slapping her clit whilst she piped me off (she had a lovely looking gash by the way). It was some night dear reader and when she left the next day I paid her the same amount that I pay the girls from a bar.

In the afternoon I had my usual routine of sitting in the pool with Greg. He was telling me that a lot of the Thai girls had told him that Thai men are no good. I can remember saying to Greg that nearly every Thai woman I'd ever spoken to had said the same to me. I told him that the bargirls had a list of lines that they say to all foreigners and that's just another one of them. (One holiday a bargirl had shown me a handbook which apparently lots of the girls carry, it's a list of phrases. One of the chapters is called 'How to get more money from Farang'!) It is impossible for all males of one particular nationality to be bad. To prove this point I said to Greg,

"If all Thai men are no good, then Thai people wouldn't exist"

There was one night that last week when Greg stayed in due to his dwindling funds. I found myself drinking alone on Soi 8 and this night I realised that Greg had absolutely made my holiday. As I walked from bar to bar I got a feeling, which I'd been having for a few nights now, that lots of the girls seemed to be pissed off with me. I honestly don't know why this was, if ever I upset people in life I usually know the reason why. I went into a bar where I know a lot of the girls and it was clear to me that I'd outstayed my welcome.

I had one drink, paid for it and got up to leave when one of the girls asked me,

"Where are you going now?"

"I'm going to go to a bar where nobody knows me."

She looked at me and said,

"Every girl on Soi 7 and Soi 8 knows you"

I laughed at the time but I knew that it wasn't supposed to be a compliment. I had spent a total of three months of that year basically just swapping between those two streets in a drunken stupor, acting like a complete slag!

After that comment I decided to go to Walking Street and by now it was 03:00 in the morning. I walked down Beach Road and as I was getting closer to the end of it I noticed lots of male prostitutes standing on it. Just when I thought I'd seen it all I saw something that I had never seen before…a white male prostitute! Trust me dear reader, I wasn't mistaken. The place he was sat and the look he gave me as I walked past left me in no doubt at all as to his reasons for being there. Sometimes you can look at people in the world and wonder what their backgrounds are. It would've been interesting to know what had happened in that man's life which had led to him being perched in that spot on Beach Road, selling his own arse.

The final week of that holiday was brilliant and I must admit that I was an absolute animal, possibly even outdoing Greg himself! When it came to the final night it became one to remember. This night was the start of the Pattaya International Fireworks Festival. There were to be firework competitions from different countries every half hour along the beach. When the first one started Greg and I were playing pool, when we finished our little tournament we took a stroll down to the beach. Almost the second our feet touched Beach Road the fireworks stopped! We headed straight back to the bar that we had just come from, telling ourselves that we'd watch the next display. When we left that bar we had crossed straight over the road to a gogo bar and by the time we left the gogo bar the firework displays had finished! Apparently those displays are one of the most impressive sights that you can see in Pattaya, they were a minute walk from where I was and I had missed them. I really am a fucking lazy bastard!

In the gogo bar that we went in was a girl that I had slept with earlier that holiday. The first time I met her she had been dancing, when she'd finished her dance she had come and sat next to me. I don't usually take gogo girls back to my room because sometimes it can be like shagging a block of wood. I never mess the girls around so I just told her that gogo girls were too expensive for me. She had told me that she could meet me in my hotel after she had finished work, that way I wouldn't have to pay the barfine and also she would accept the same pay as a bargirl. Her body was amazing so the agreement was made and kept.

When I had walked in there again on my final night she had come straight up to me and told me that she would meet me in my room again at 03:00, I agreed. When Greg and I left that bar it was just after midnight. I told Greg about the arrangement and told him that I wanted to have short-time with someone else before she came to my room. What would happen this night would turn it into the most surreal night that I've ever had in that city.

I stuck to my plan and picked up a girl and took her back to my room to have some pretty forgettable sex. After she left I just passed out. At 03:00 I was awoken by a knock on the door, it was the gogo girl. I let her in and then immediately got back into bed and fell asleep. I don't want to sound nasty here but when I had met this girl the first time she had seemed nice but she definitely wasn't the *'sharpest tool in the toolbox'*.

I can remember waking up at one point and she was cuddled tightly into me and bizarrely I was cuddling her! (I'm not usually the cuddling type) She was talking to me and I can remember just nodding and falling back to sleep. When I woke up properly it was 04:30. I honestly don't know what had been going on when I'd been laid in an unconscious state, but now that I was awake it seemed that all sorts of arrangements had been made between us! She told me that we were boyfriend and girlfriend and that I was coming to see her house in six days' time!

I laid there with my brain absolutely fried! My head was already fucked from the whisky and the nap and I laid there not having a clue what was going on. Dear reader, I know for a fact that I had been flat out asleep whilst she had been in the room. What she had been doing it that time I would love to know, I wish I had been a fly on the wall. Had she been laid next to me, talking to me and asking me questions for the entire time? I honestly think she had.

I got up and had a shower to wake myself up a bit, then I had a smoke and after that I sat her down. I was feeling confused, uncomfortable and I was also starting to feel very guilty...even though I hadn't done anything wrong! I told her that I was going back to England later that day and that I wouldn't be coming back for a while. She looked disappointed and a bit confused herself. After this little chat I got her to ride me and then I fell straight back to sleep, making sure my side of the bed was kept to myself.

When I awoke in the early afternoon of my final day, it was time for her to go but I had a hard time getting her out of my room. She asked me if she could come to the airport with me, I said no. She asked if she could wait with me until the taxi came and I told her she couldn't because I needed to say goodbye to some people. She then asked if she could wait in my room whilst I was out and again I said no. The last question she asked me was if I had a pen to write her number down...I lied and said I didn't. She told me that she would leave her number with reception. From first asking her to leave to her actually going took over one hour, I've got a heart of stone but I'm not ill-mannered.

I had a few hours in the pool with Greg and then I went and packed my suitcase. Greg actually came and sat in the reception with me whilst I waited for my taxi, which was kind of him. When I had first walked into the reception the girl behind the desk had handed me a note. It was from the gogo girl, at the top was her name, below that her phone number and below that were three words...'*I LOVE YOU*'. I threw it straight in the bin. Am I a bad man dear reader? I promise you that I don't mean to be.

I know for definite now that I will never beat my first ever holiday in Pattaya, but this fifth holiday had come as close as it's possible to get. I'd slept with more women than any other holiday, I'd had sex more times than any other holiday, I'd had the solo experience, the girlfriend experience and most importantly of all the Greg experience. What a fucking holiday! One month like that each year and I'll die a happy man!

CHAPTER THREE

INTO THE VOID

1

The first three days back at home my body felt completely broken and I barely used my feet. But I wasn't laid sulking, I kept my mind busy by writing. Everything you have just read (minus the introduction) is a product of those three days. Writing everything down on paper first and then typing it all up on a laptop. To my surprise that first week was nowhere near as bad as what it should've been. In life I'm a pessimist but sometimes I can completely surprise myself with my own positive thinking. I wasn't thinking of how I could get back to Thailand, I was just concentrating on fixing things.

By the end of the week I had smoothed over all the family problems that I'd had. Don't worry bad luck kept coming thick and fast but I didn't let it bother me…there was absolutely no work about and I had to spend £300, which I really didn't have, on car repairs.

I think my optimism that first week came from the fact that I'd just had one of the best months of my entire life. No matter what pain laid in front of me I had absolutely *no* regrets whatsoever!

In the following weeks boredom was setting in. I had nothing to write and no money to spend. I sent my second book off to the publisher so that he could begin the formatting process. During this time I felt compelled to write a new chapter for it. The inspiration came from the news reports that I had been watching in the last couple of days, a Muslim had taken some Aussies hostage in a café in Sydney and the Taliban had massacred a load of school kids in Pakistan! That chapter was 'Islam Ramadana Ding Dong'. I showed it to a mate at the time and he told me I could end up being thrown in prison. I remember saying to him,

"Good! I'd end up being a millionaire and I'd have an interesting prison chapter for my new book!"

As Christmas rapidly approached my optimism left me. The news reports were saying that the North Sea Oil Industry was on the verge of collapse due to plummeting oil prices. All around me other men were being paid off which meant more competition for any jobs that were starting. Then luckily on Christmas Eve I received a phone call offering me one week's work offshore, it would be just enough to keep my finances in the black.

A boring cunt might say that the end of a year is a time to reflect. As 2014 drew to a close I looked back upon it and realised how lucky I had been. Although September 2013 to August 2014 had been the best twelve month period of my life, the year 2014 was easily the best year of my life so far. I had only worked fourteen weeks, I had spent three months in Thailand and I had written two books after discovering a new found hobby. I knew that I had been lucky and I was grateful for it, but on the other hand I couldn't help feeling slightly depressed. How long will I have to wait to have another year like that one? Will I ever have another year like that one?

On Tuesday 6th January 2015 I sent my final draft of Rigs, Pigs & Dirty Digs off to the publisher. I had amended all the mistakes I could see and I'd also added a few extra mildly amusing comments for good measure. On Wednesday 7th January 2015 eight journalists and four other people were brutally murdered by Muslim extremists in a magazine headquarters in the centre of Paris. As the news story unfolded my initial thoughts were, *'What the fuck have I done?'* As the day progressed I realised that now more than ever should free speech be protected and more importantly Islam should be ridiculed. (Plus luckily for me there's a real bloke with my pen name and he's from the adjoining county to my own! If there's ever a Barry J Steel jihadist beheading video then hopefully it's him in it rather than me!)

In that second book I had written that in times of Islamic terror attacks we never really see these so called Muslim moderates speak out. On the day of the Paris attacks I pretty much just left the BBC News channel on the telly. I only saw one interview with a Muslim all day long. He was 'English' and he only spoke for two minutes, obviously he condemned the attacks but he also couldn't resist attacking the French cartoons as well! These cartoonist's had only been dead for a few hours! I had to laugh over the fact that the ultra-left-wing and staunch supporter of multiculturalism, BBC could only manage to get their hands on this idiot. It cemented everything that I had written! I watched that news story with utter disgust like everyone else in western society. I dare say that I felt the disgust even more than your average man due to the content of my book. A brand new year and even more religious violence to start it off.

I'm going to say something that I'm not allowed to say but this statement really needs to be said! You CANNOT be both Muslim and English, you are either one or the other. The cultures are just far *too* different from one another. I understand that the young Muslims born in England today will feel like outcasts in our society and for that I feel sorry for them. BUT I was raised Christian and if I can question everything and educate myself and realise that *all* religion is bullshit then everyone can! Embrace the culture of the country you are born in, NOT the culture of the country that your parents left behind!

This is what it means to be English…you are really good at queuing, you are overly polite (in a restaurant you will moan about the food and service behind a waiters back but compliment him to his face), you love pork sausages, you love the countryside, you have a love for alcohol and most importantly of all, you can laugh at yourself! That is the English culture regardless of what ignorant do-gooders tell us! If you kneel down on a mat and pray to Allah everyday then you are *not* fucking English!

2

The next few months after that terrorist incident were a living hell for me. Although my second book was released in this period (we'll save that for another chapter) in the real world life was pretty unpleasant. No money, no work and living in a half-finished house. Each day was a mundane chore, ringing companies, sending out CV's. I was *that* bored sometimes I would have two baths a day just to give me something to do. I also found that I was masturbating profusely. (It was around this time that I *stumbled* upon a porn video with a midget in it. Just when I thought my spirits couldn't be crushed any further it turned out I was wrong. I was absolutely devastated to see that this midget's dick was a lot bigger than mine!)

I would do the school run, always struggling to pick out my own kids from the sea of similar faces. Then I would take them home and get annoyed by the children's programmes they'd watch on the telly!

There's something you need to know about me dear reader, when I was a kid I was happy and all I ever wanted to do was make the people around me laugh. When the harsh reality of life slapped me in the face in my late teens I lost some of my spark. Life kept grinding me down more and more over the years. When my ex-wife and I bought a house together, bringing a list of bills, my sense of humour completely changed. I found that I would now 'humorously' moan about different things. Eventually one day my ex said to me,

"All you do is fucking moan!"

I realised that she was right. The humour had slowly disappeared from my moaning and I realised that life had turned me into the miserable bastard that I am today. After my kids were born I found that there were lots more things in life to moan about, children's TV being one of them!

I hate all forms of propaganda but I especially hate the propaganda being forced down our kids throats every day by the BBC! Multiculturalism is a failed experiment, our Prime Minister David Cameron admitted this and so did the most powerful and respected woman in the world, the German Chancellor Angela Merkel. The BBC refuse to admit this fact though and they constantly herald multiculturalism as great success rather than the segregated, racist mess that it really is.

When I turned on the telly one day and saw a kids programme called 'Rastamouse' I felt like punching the screen. My wife actually had to tell me to shut up and calm down! This programme is about Rastafarian mice with strong Caribbean accents. Does the thick BBC not realise that Rastafarianism is a religion and the biggest component of it is the spiritual smoking of cannabis? Why aren't these mice walking around smoking spliff's? They all sound stoned so why not show them getting stoned?! The BBC can't keep hand picking little bits from each culture, leaving out the bad bits, forcing them into our kid's brains whilst slowly eroding our own culture at the same time!

3

During this period it wasn't *completely* quiet work wise. An offshore job that I was promised in January was put on hold at the last minute and then the exact same thing happened to me again in February. That's just the nature of offshore though. Also a horrendous sounding job came up. An onshore job…

I have a list of cities that I have absolutely no intention of ever visiting in my lifetime. Level pegging with Bagdad is the city of Belfast…deemed one of the most dangerous places on earth during the 1970's. In February a shit paid job came up in this city and with my back against the wall I had no option but to put my CV forward for it. Numerous agencies were recruiting for the job and I put my CV in with a few of them. One of them sent me out a load of forms to fill in and sign, they were the usual shite except for one big glaring question…they wanted to know if I was A) Protestant B) Catholic C) Other. It's a question I've never seen before and I really couldn't believe that a UK company in 2015 was asking me it! It should be fucking illegal!

Even though I was desperate at the time there was absolutely no way that I was going to lie and tick Protestant. (My pride and honesty have always set me back in life!) Ticking Catholic would almost certainly have meant that my CV would either be thrown out or put to the bottom of the pile. I don't consider myself to be Catholic anyway so I didn't tick that box either. Instead I ticked Other and scribbled in Atheist. That must have offended those thick cunts more than anything else because I never did get a reply! It's not a very Christian attitude those micks seem to have is it dear reader? Put it this way, I would rather lay in front of a mirror and fist myself than apply for a job in that backwards shithole again!

So this was my life at the time, boredom, frustration, anger and absolutely skint. Whilst doing that one week's offshore over New Year I had joined a jobsite called LinkedIn. I was checking it ten times a day. I noticed straight away that for a person to get a job in recruitment they have to be A) a woman and B) a stunner! I have to pay tribute to their shallow male bosses, good choice men!

I already know that there's lots of snivelling cunts within my industry but I saw a photo on that site that made my jaw hang slack in disbelief! The photo was of some manager sat in his office chair and he was thanking the lads for all the Christmas presents they'd sent in! He was sat there with gifts on his knees and in one hand was a bottle of Glenmorangie! Who are these wretches? If you are reading this and you are one of these 'men' who send in cards and presents to the office staff then I have a message for you.....hang your fucking head in shame!

I soon realised what that jobsite was for, it wasn't for jobs at all! It was for bored office staff, who have no life outside of their work, to post 'profound' quotes that had been made by billionaire businessmen, which serve absolutely no purpose in life! And also it's for spineless men with absolutely no dignity to unashamedly congratulate and suck up to them.

I can tell you that it's a very hard pill to swallow this unemployment bollocks. One minute I'm living like a jetsetter, swanning off to Thailand for one month long holidays whenever I felt like it. Then the next minute I'm destitute and can't even afford the petrol to have a day out in Redcar! It's just part of the game unfortunately. I'd written in my second book that a contractor's life can be feast or famine and here I was, a few months after writing those words, the living proof of it.

When March arrived with no sign of any work I was a lot calmer than what I deserved to be. If I had still been married I would have been an absolute dithering wreck by now but luckily divorce changes a man. The biggest fear in any man's life (outside of family health) is losing his home. When you get divorced that's just part of the package. When you manage to get through it and realise everything is still OK then it's like conquering a fear. I suppose of all the changes that divorce brings the biggest one to me is that I no longer abuse myself in the toilets at work. I just don't feel the need to anymore. Sometimes I really miss those double-time Sunday wanks.

In mid-march I finally caved in and signed on the dole, it had been something I was hoping to avoid doing. The degrading process a person has to go through to get their £75 a week doesn't seem worth it. I don't like stuck up low paid idiots looking down their nose at me and I don't like being interrogated for ten minutes whilst the scumbag next to me just has to sign a box and pick up his money with no questions asked.

I was dismayed to find out two new changes had occurred since I last signed on. You have to sign on every week now instead of once a fortnight and even worse your council tax is no longer automatically paid! You have to go grovelling to your local council office and beg them for help. When I first signed on I did actually ask the man in the jobcentre,

"At what point will you start paying my bills?"

"We don't. Just the interest on your mortgage."

I didn't ask him anything else but I did wonder to myself how some people manage to live on the dole. It's impossible that these people survive on £75 a week and only their rent paid. How do these people pay energy bills, insurances and everything else? I can only assume that when you're a higher band tax payer like myself then there are many hidden benefits that you aren't entitled to. If those Scandinavians saw the way our welfare system treats honest working citizens they would think of us as barbarians! We have to give praise to Maggie Thatcher for this, she kindly scrapped income based benefits!

By now I had cut back on *everything*! I was living on a diet that mainly consisted of ham sandwiches and beans on toast. Using ASDA's Smart Price Range I managed to cut down my weekly food bill to £20! (I'm not exaggerating about the beans on toast!) I would feel ashamed whilst I stood at the till and then I would be quietly annoyed by the obese checkout workers when they would robotically ask me if I was capable of packing my own bags! I had to cut back on my boiler usage, the luxury of having baths was replaced with a quick shower and I even cut back on masturbation. Whether my diet had completely killed off my libido or I was conscious of wasting sperm I'm not really sure.

It's a shit society we live in when money worries supersede every other problem in a person's life. Those wankers who say, '*Money doesn't make you happy*' are fucking idiots. Money relieves the stresses and burdens of everyday life. That might be a sad fact but it's also a true fact. I realised during this time that you need money to have *any* sort of enjoyment in life.

Even a walk in the countryside still costs the price of the petrol you need to get you there. With absolutely no money I can honestly say that by this point in my life having a poo became the highlight of my day!

I had been paid off at the end of October and I finally got the call for a job at the very end of March. In all that time I had only managed to get one week's work! Although we can discount the month I had in Thailand, never the less this was still the worst bout of unemployment that I have ever had. I must give some credit to Barack Obama and the American government for manipulating the oil prices just to have a dig at Russia. That selfish act affected millions of people across the planet! I would love to see that wanker living on beans on toast!

I had lost almost five irreplaceable months of my life and all my plans for the year had been ruined. I had spent every last penny of my savings, I was maxed out on an overdraft and I was in debt to my parents for the first time in my adult life! It's the worst financial situation that I have ever been in.

You have no idea what a relief it is for me to finish writing this horrible fucking chapter. I have never been so happy to have a job in all my life! And the best thing about this job was that I was going to finally escape from that place that had held me prisoner all winter long...Teesside.

CHAPTER FOUR

TEESSIDE...A LOVER'S PARADISE

Teesside is an area in the North East of England that most people have never heard of. The rest of our cousins in the North East have given us two nicknames, 'The Nappy Rippers' which comes from some big paedophile scandal in the 1980's and the more popular nickname 'Smoggies'. The reason we have been labelled Smoggies comes from the vast amount of industry in our area. An endless sight of cooling towers and chimneys fill our skies with shite. It's a nickname that we have embraced.

If anyone wanted to visit our lovely area they would have to get onto the A1 motorway travelling northbound and then take the A19 exit. A stranger travelling along the A19 will be struck by the surrounding beauty, the North York Moors on your right and rolling countryside to the left. When you reach Teesside you will immediately know about it, the motorway widens, cooling towers appear on the horizon in front of you and you will also be hit by a smell. The smell isn't from the industry, it comes from the town of Thornaby on the left hand side. An outsider is advised to steer well clear of this place, the half-evolved knuckle dragging occupants who live there don't give a very warm welcome.

As you carry on up the motorway you will soon be on the Tees flyover. Teesside gets its name from the River Tees which flows right through the middle of this land. (To anyone childishly sniggering at our rivers name, I can promise you there is nothing flirtatious about it) As the motorway crosses the river you are elevated to a height of around 60 Ft and from here you get to see Teesside in all its glory. On your left, heavenly beams of sunlight will be shining down on the town of Stockton. On your right there's a shitty little patch of waste-ground called Middlesbrough and behind that is the sight of all the vast industry. Anyone who has a love for chemical plants and factories will no doubt think it's a spectacular view…however to normal people it will look like hell on earth.

Like anywhere else in the world there is good and bad. Our good areas are very nice and someone from the south of England would be shocked to learn that they could trade in their shitty two bed terraced house for a 4 bed detached up here. We are spoilt rotten with the surrounding countryside and most areas in Teesside have a view of the picturesque Cleveland Hills.

We have a bit of a strange accent, English people think we sound like Geordies and foreigners think we are Irish. Makem's and Geordies call us the North East Scouser's because we use similar slang words to those poor unfortunates who live in Liverpool.

When it comes to claims to fame we can't compete with the big cities because we are merely a collection of small towns. But the friction match was invented in Teesside, the world's first passenger railway line is in Teesside and to all you boring vegetarian tits out there, we gave you Quorn. Both the Sydney Harbour and Tyne bridges were built in Teesside. Our most famous human exports are Captain James Cook, the musicians Paul Rogers and Chris Rea, the comedians Bob Mortimer and Roy 'Chubby' Brown and also unfortunately for us the magician Paul Daniels. The film directors Tony and Ridley Scott also grew up here. Anyone who has seen the thoroughly depressing film Blade Runner should know that the opening shot of that film was inspired by Teesside's industrial skyline.

Growing up in Teesside I had a brilliant childhood, the estate I lived in was surrounded by countryside and building sites…a young boys dream. Then when I hit my late teens I grew to hate the place, classing it as a shithole with absolutely nothing to do. But I would imagine that even the teenagers in the big cities have exactly the same feelings. As I've gotten older I've grown to really appreciate where I live. Like I've already said we are a stone's throw away from beautiful scenery, country villages and nice beaches (Saltburn NOT Redcar!). We also have some of the cheapest houses in the country. When I see the debt that southerners get into just for modest sized houses, I struggle to comprehend how they survive. A southern tradesman doesn't earn any more money than a northern tradesman, so the excuse of 'difference in wages' doesn't come into it.

In my own line of work Teessiders are like fucking rats…we are absolutely everywhere! I have never been on a job that didn't have Smoggies on it. A few people have asked me over the years, '*Why are there so many of you?*' Just go onto Google Images and type in the words 'Teesside Industry' and that question is immediately answered.

Because there are so many of us on jobs we don't all cling to each other like people from other areas do (Scouser's are notorious for doing this). I personally don't care where my workmates are from and I have a massive pet-hatred when it comes to Smoggies. The largest town in Teesside is called Middlesbrough and people from there class themselves as being from '*The Boro*' which is pronounced '*The Buro*'. I've found that a lot of Teessiders who aren't actually from Middlesbrough also class themselves as being from 'The Buro'. Like so many things in life this really pisses me off and as usual I don't really understand the reason why. If someone asks me where I'm from I will always say, 'Teesside' and the usual reply to that is,

"So you're from the Buro then?"

I have bitten the head off many a man for saying that to me!

Unfortunately for us, although our industry is vast it doesn't support all the contractors it has produced. When new jobs do start these days they are usually flooded with cheap foreign labour meaning we are forced to travel the land, working in everyone else's area. (Most people in Britain don't get to hear the stories of British workers getting pushed out of their own areas by foreigners. This is due to a media blackout first introduced by that fucking useless blind arsehole Gordon Brown!)

When I started this new job I would once again find myself becoming part of that detested bunch of men…The Teesside Mafia!

CHAPTER FIVE

A RETURN TO THE MUG'S LIFE

1

Sometimes in life there's only one thing worse than unemployment…it's the phone call telling you that you've got a job. The reason for this is because some of the jobs within my industry can be so horrendous, you really, really don't want to do them. Turning down shit jobs is a luxury we take for granted in the summer months but in those quiet times when our backs are against the wall, we really can't say no. That horrible sleepless night before you're due to start…with a pile of losing scratch cards on your bedside table.

Every aspect of life has a hierarchy and the construction industry is no different. The hierarchy of my world is as follows:
(Please note I have never worked in a shipyard or on a nuclear so I cannot comment on them. Also I

understand that there are always exceptions to the rule, so not everyone might agree with me here)

FAB-SHOPS- These are modern day workhouses, where men allow themselves to be treated like animals day in day out. They are bullied all day long by a management who constantly spy on them and harass them. Any man who talks to a work colleague for longer than thirty seconds will instantly be approached and asked, '*What's the hold up?*' For this wonderful treatment the men are paid low wages which just about allows them to survive. The surroundings are bleak and depressing, the noise is unbearable and some of these places are extremely dangerous! I have absolutely no sympathy at all for the 'men' who choose to stay in this environment. You have never seen genuine fear until you have looked into the eyes of a fab-shop monkey after he's just heard the word 'payoffs'.

RIG YARDS- In rig yards men can earn good wages and a practice of Health & Safety means that they aren't driven by a whip hand like their counterparts in the fab-shops. These men aren't harassed *but* they are spied on from a distance. The surroundings are equally as unpleasant as a fab-shop though, meaning these are soul destroying places to drive to each day. I have seen grown men running and hiding from foremen in these places!

POWERSTATIONS- These are a huge leap up from the rig yards. The sheer size of these places means that men cannot be spied on all day long. Outside of shutdown season these are very relaxed places to work in. Men will fill most of their day swapping stories and drawing penises. When the shutdowns do start however the environment quickly changes. The site gets flooded with men who are forced to crawl all over each other like ants! Some of the filthy, awkward shitholes that a man will have to work in means the day can be long and unpleasant.

CHEMICAL PLANTS- Again these are huge places, some of them being the size of small towns! The bigger the site, the more relaxed the atmosphere. The Health & Safety is *so* strict in these places that it's almost impossible for a man to be worked to the bone. The only downside to chemical plants is the weather conditions men will have to work in. In the freezing winter months on an outside job, you can miss a roof being over your head.

If we go back to the fab-shops, I must admit that I've got a couple of fond memories from working in these places. You'll find that when men are treated like children, some of them will act like children…myself included.

When I was in my early twenties I had a spell working in a fab-shop, but it was one of the larger ones. Working with two *real* friends meant that fun could be had in this place. To lighten the mood of the daily grind pranks would be pulled. The welders would have their sets turned off mid-weld, toolboxes would be vandalised, homosexual graffiti about work colleagues and management would be written on the toilet walls, rumours of payoffs would be started and of course there was the obligatory drawing of penises…be it on walls or on people's backs.

I may possibly hold a world record dear reader! In this particular fab-shop we were building a bridge and each of the section beams were thirty feet long. In a moment of pure boredom I decided to draw a cock on the full length of one of these beams. Later in the shift I was talking within a small group of men and I had completely forgotten about my childish act from earlier. Suddenly one of the men in our little group burst out laughing and pointed upwards. When I turned to see what he was laughing at I was delighted to find that it was the beam I had defaced. Two cranes had hoisted it right up in the air and it was now travelling down the full length of the shop. I sniggered to myself as I watched all my work colleagues stop what they were doing and stare in awe at a huge thirty foot cock passing above their heads!

I might get in touch with the Guinness Book Of World Records and ask them what's the biggest childish knob that's ever been drawn?

Luckily for me it's been a number of years since I've had to work in a fab-shop now. (Sometimes they're a necessary evil) There are two men from that last hell-hole who I will never forget. Both these men were a similar age to me but we were all very different from each other. I had been working on the nightshift at this place and nightshift is something I always prefer when I'm working onshore. (You will hear men say that nightshift is only for burglars and rapists! I find this statement to be quite unfounded and also I've noticed its only borderline alcoholics who spend every night in the pub who say it. The extra money that nightshift brings means I generally don't feel the need to burgle people's homes. Also after a nightshift I find that I'm just too tired to drive straight to a park and force someone to have sex with me. Nightshift to me means more money, sleep-ins, long weekends off and a more relaxed working environment)

The first man, from this fab-shop, was one of the nicest men that I have ever met and he was also very intelligent. This man had worked in fab-shops his entire life, never working away from home once, but sometimes having to travel long distances day in and day out. I can remember asking him why he had settled for this lifestyle. A man as nice and as clever as him deserved a better life. He told me that his father had worked offshore his whole life and it had upset him as a boy for his dad to keep disappearing all the time. He said that he didn't want his young son to go through what he'd had to go through. (I almost felt like giving him a cuddle) A noble reason I'm sure you'd all agree. I couldn't do it myself though.

The second man was the complete opposite. He was big, thick and a fucking idiot! (If you have read the book Animal Farm, this man was Boxer the horse!) He would do the work of two men all day long without any thought for his own health and safety and doing any job the foreman asked of him. A couple of weeks after I'd started he was made up to charge-hand and he became the horrible bully I'd already sussed him out to be. I've noticed that people like him always have the same mind-set. When they're on the tools they see anyone who works as hard as they do as a threat! Then when they get made up they expect everyone to work like they had done! They really are fucking lunatics!

Before he was made up I was stood watching him one day. He was grinding thick rust from a load of steel, without wearing any gloves or respiratory equipment. When he took a rare five second breather I approached him and had a chat with him.

"Do you know mate, a *very* rich man once said, '*a little hard work never hurt anyone*' but the fact is a *lot* of hard work knocks years off your life?"

When I said this to him he looked at me as if I was a little bit mental and he replied with this,

"When I go, I go, I don't really give a fuck."

From that moment on we hated each other. He labelled me a lazy bastard and I labelled him a thick cunt who didn't deserve a life. When he was 'made up' we constantly argued but luckily for me I soon found a proper job. Workmates are like family…you can't choose them!

2

Anyone reading this who doesn't work in my industry will find the remainder of this chapter completely alien to them. I promise that there is nothing unusual in what you are about to read, this is simply the world that we contractors live in. Unfortunately for us, everything you are about to read is *very* usual.

When I finally got the call for a job in March I was lucky in the fact that it was for a chemical plant. By then all my delusions about staying offshore had vanished and I was just happy to be back in work (any job would've made me happy at that point in my life, even a fab-shop! I had been a couple of weeks away from standing in the street and selling myself!). However the short notice I was given for the job was ridiculous! I got the call at 12:30 and was told I had to start the very next day. If the job had been on my doorstep it wouldn't have been a problem but this job wasn't on my doorstep, it was in one of the most inhospitable places in the British Isles and to get there I would be using planes, trains and automobiles! Although I'll never explicitly tell you what sites/rigs I've worked on, I think the majority of you reading this will have already figured out which job I'm talking about here.

When I first stepped off the plane I thought someone had played a big joke on me. Then it sank in, it wasn't a joke at all, it was real! I had just landed on the bleakest, most depressing landscape that I had ever seen in my life! (And I've been to Birkenhead) This place literally looked like Satan himself had crawled up from the bowels of hell and had a massive shit in the middle of the sea!

As I boarded the coach, that was taking me to my new temporary home, I was hit by the wind! I think wind must have been invented in this place because there wasn't a day in my whole time there that it wasn't blowing. As the coach made the journey I looked out onto the barren, desolate land. My secret hobby of making love to trees would have to be put on hold during my time up here.

I got talking about offshore with the man sat next to me and he told me one of those typical offshore stories that you hear every now and again. He told me this story was about his mate but I suspected it was just a story that he had heard.

Apparently there was a man who would take a dozen oranges offshore with him on every trip. This is quite a peculiar habit because every rig has an abundance of oranges on them. Obviously this man had a reason to why he was so particular about his own oranges…he would use a syringe to inject each one of them with vodka! Each night after shift he would be seen sat in the TV lounge sucking on an orange. After a time he was stopped in the heliport by suspicious jobsworth security staff. Maybe they were just curious but it's more than likely that he had been bladed by a fellow co-worker. He was caught red handed and lost his job on the spot. Any man who has to go to those lengths to have a drink has a very serious problem!

When the coach arrived at the camp, it turned out to be better than what I'd thought. In my mind I had pictured a military style base but it was just the same as living on an oil rig. There were two differences between this camp and a rig though, this place had a bar and also a prayer room. Dear reader, I fucking hate prayer rooms! The way that companies pander to these religious nutjobs really pisses me off! Companies never want to pander to me! Porn is my religion, why can't we have a masturbation room?

When I started on site the next day I received a shock. The amount of foreign labour on the job was absolutely staggering! Now I've got nothing personal against the foreigners, after all they are just men like me trying to earn a living and I myself have worked abroad. But I couldn't help feeling pissed off that I had been allowed to sit unemployed for such a long time. I really wanted to write VOTE UKIP in big lettering on the back of my jacket and in my younger days I would have done it without thinking twice.

We need a common sense approach to the use of foreign labour. They should only be used when British labour has been exhausted, and as soon as a Brit signs on the dole a foreigner needs to be given a tap on his shoulder and told to make way. And those ignorant fucking bastards who say *'Europeans work harder than the British'* that is a complete fallacy! I have seen it with my own eyes! The vast majority of them work at exactly the same pace as us and the few who do work harder are only able to do so by breaking every single Health & Safety Law that this country has ever produced! It is usual to see these animals climbing over handrails, using ladders three at a time and tampering with scaffolding! These do-gooders who spout that shite should be ashamed of themselves! The British have always been known as a nation of hard workers who work longer hours than the rest of Europe. Then the pro-immigration propaganda machine started and the British working classes found themselves indistinguishable from the 'Scrounging Class'. These do-gooders are more dangerous to their fellow countrymen than fucking terrorists! I've noticed that they're never in jobs that are affected by foreign labour, I would love to see what tune they sang if they turned up for work tomorrow to be told that they were being replaced by a cheaper Polish worker!

3

When you work on a large site the strict Health & Safety procedures means there is usually lots of downtime. It's that age old saying, *'The more you earn the less you do'*. When the management are capable and organised then the job can be very good. When men are facing a long spell of downtime they will be told to go and sit in the cabin until they are needed. As well as being a good practise of Health & Safety this also keeps the men happy. A happy workforce is a more productive workforce. (You will never see men work as fast when they know there's a chair and cup of tea waiting for them once the work is complete) If the job should fall behind for whatever reason then the tried and tested method of *'job and knock'* never fails.

On a badly ran job the difference is incredible! There are many reasons why a management can be disorganised...clashing egos, underqualified men getting jobs through their father-in-law etc. The downtime becomes a bit of a joke and as the job starts to fall behind the management will make life hell for the lads. They are so blinded by their own incompetence that they will always blame the tradesmen.

The first thing they will introduce is very strict break times and when they realise that strict breaks has absolutely no effect on production they take it to the next level. They hire in 'policemen', this isn't their official job title but that's basically all that they are. These men are usually retired managers who had a reputation for bullying. They are paid a *lot* of money to walk around site looking for idle men and guarding the cabins at break times.

Men will only ever stand idle when they haven't been allocated a job or if they cannot get on with their task for whatever valid reason. They are never stood idle through laziness, it's just through pure bad management. When the policemen approach them then they will pointlessly pretend to be busy like little fucking children! When these old wankers get a bit tired of walking around bullying people or if the weather has a turn for the worse then they will slope off to a comfy chair in a nice warm cabin. The men they have just bullied will have no such luxury though, they are forced to stand on site with nothing to do except being a hazard! The hypocrisy fucking stinks! All these policemen achieve is costing companies a lot of money in wages and infuriating a workforce. Pissed off tradesmen will just leave looking for better jobs, meaning the company will have to waste even more money on training and inducting new employees. If a site is full of idle men then it is a clear sign that *management* needs to be changed. That never happens though, it will always be *our* fault!

One huge problem in my industry these days are managers who just don't belong in it. They come from a world of managing office staff in permanent jobs and they believe that they can treat contractors in exactly the same way. But we aren't office staff and we never have permanent jobs, therefore our mentality is completely different. If a job is shit we just leave and get a better one! These *outsider* managers don't understand the concept of something like 'job and knock' so they introduce finger print clocking machines to try and eradicate it. They do not realise that ultimately all they are doing is shaving a lot of money off their own bonuses!

I realised that this new job of mine was badly organised straight away, the policemen were there, the breaks were strict and they even had a no smoking in work time policy! In my first four shifts I only completed around two hour's work. My foreman wouldn't cabin me up out of fear, so he would simply tell me to either hide or to look busy. I think the reason for the mismanagement on this job was purely down to lack of communication and I believe that the sheer number of nationalities on site was the biggest factor in this. We were told in our induction that there were around 20 different nationalities on the job!

The treatment of the men was pretty shit and in my second week there I heard a story which absolutely horrified me. Just before I had started a man had had a heart attack on site, his two fellow co-workers immediately began to resuscitate him until an ambulance arrived. Once the professionals took over they were approached by a manager. The usual treatment for a couple of heroes like this would be to sit them down with a cup of tea, make sure they were okay and then send them home. Unfortunately for these two men this manager was an Arab. He didn't even ask them if they were okay, he simply said,

"You two go back to work now."

When they refused he tried to have them disciplined! Forgive me if the next line sounds mildly racist but as I'm writing this my blood is boiling! That dirty, horrible camel-raping wanker should've been sacked on the spot, deported and banned from our kingdom for life! We don't want a backwards Third World mentality on our jobs and we certainly don't want these men in charge of us!

Stories like that one would have set me off on a path to self-destruction in my past but I've managed to get a grip on my work related anger issues these days. Older colleagues would constantly tell me '*Just play the game son*' but I never could. These days I'm an expert at playing this silly little game. As one very old colleague once told me,

"Just piss up their backs!"

Luckily I was soon put onto the nightshift where I was treated like a man and kept away from these horror stories.

4

Both the best and worst thing about my industry are the people I have to work with. If you stand five work colleagues in front of me, one will be a wretch, one will be a dickhead, one will be nice but boring and two will be men who I can genuinely get along with.

If you stick five strangers together the loudest man in the group will usually be the wretch. These men never know when to keep their fucking mouths shut! There are many reasons why I might label a man a dickhead. A brief example from this job would be two men I overheard talking one morning whilst I was stood in a queue waiting for a coach. They were chatting about another colleague who didn't have the privilege of knowing he was being talked about. Listening to men slag off their workmates is nothing new but this conversation was a little bit different from the norm. They were actually discussing the brand of trainers that this man would wear! If two grown men are thick enough to have a conversation about another man's footwear then it instantly tells me that they are devoid of both intelligence and any real personality. These are the type of men who I would label dickheads.

You get to meet people from all walks of life in my industry. I have worked with many ex-criminals who were unlucky in having a bad start in life and more often than not they are pure gentlemen. You also get to meet many 'characters'. These can be extremely funny men and also extremely strange men.

On this job I got paired up with a man who within forty minutes of meeting him admitted to me that he was a sadomasochist! I would describe myself as an unshockable person but the stuff this man told me shocked me. He spent the best part of twenty minutes telling me the different ways he would torture very willing women. Trust me dear reader, the stuff he told me is too morbid even for one of my books. There was one man who told me a perverted story which is a bit more suited to my pages though.

This man had once worked with a swinger and this swinger would take great delight in telling his workmates what he would get up to in his spare time. There was one night he had taken a drive thirty miles north from his home. He was off to meet a couple who he had met online. This was on a work night and he drove up there stone cold sober. (I'm guessing he has a dick like a grand piano leg!) When he arrived at the couple's house he was invited in and the three of them sat in the front room and had a cup of tea together. The swinger had described this as a sort of informal 'interview'. Before too long he was banging this man's wife on the front room carpet right in front of him. The husband then took out his penis and began to masturbate. Please keep in mind that the swinger at the centre of this story was happily telling anyone at work who would listen! So he's nailing this woman and the excitement of it all has the desired effect on the husband. He shot his manfat all over the swingers back!

When I hear stories like this one I have to question if I really have the right to call myself a pervert. I think at best I'm just a filthy slag.

In my last book I told you the 'Mrs Jones Joke', one of the most offensive jokes on the planet. (By the way, did any of you spot the glaring spelling mistake in the title?) I decided to tell this joke to the man who told me the swinger story. It had the desired effect and he then told me that he had his own favourite sick joke and he proceeded to tell me it. As I braced myself for an awkward silence I surprisingly found myself laughing out loud. Because I hadn't heard this one before I'm putting it in this book, but for all I know it might be quite popular so my apologies if you already know it.

Its Christmas time and little nine year old Sarah is sat on Santa's knee in the grotto,
Santa- "Ho, Ho, Ho! What would you like for Christmas this year Sarah?"
Sarah is shy and nervously says to Santa,
Sarah- "W-w-well S-S-Santa…some of the girls in my class have s-s-started to get hairs in-between their l-l-legs…"
Santa's eyes immediately lit up,
Santa- "Yes Sarah, don't be shy."

Sarah- "W-w-well Santa, I was w-w-wondering if for Christmas this year, I could have h-h-hairs in-between my legs as well?"

Santa stared at the shy little girl, leaned in closer and whilst licking his lips he said,

Santa- "Sarah…will a white beard do?"

5

The rotation for this job was three weeks on and one week off. When I first arrived on site I was told that I would only be getting two trips and if I wanted to work right through then I could. The most consecutive shifts that I had ever worked in the past was 21 and for a man who loves time off as much as me this had been more than enough. But after sitting on my arse for so long and starting this job absolutely penniless I felt up for the challenge. So I started a marathon run that would eventually turn out to be 56 consecutive shifts worked! If someone had told me at the start of the year that I was going to do this I never would have believed them. (There are tradesmen in Britain right now working a *lot* more than this!)

I soon realised a problem though, for the first time in my life I was going to miss my vote in the upcoming general election. If Labour were to regain power and I hadn't done my tiny little bit to try and prevent it then I never would have forgiven myself. I got in touch with my local council and they kindly agreed to send my postal vote up to the island for me.

I told numerous work colleagues that I had done this and the majority of them seemed completely disinterested. Most of them were missing their vote but they didn't care, however nearly every shift I would have to sit and listen to them moaning on about the foreigners. Men never seem to want to help themselves!

As the job progressed I began to lose all track of time. The few hours I would have to myself each day before my shift began would be spent walking around in a zombified state. I remember sitting with a colleague and telling him that five weeks up here was starting to take its toll on me. He then pointed out to me that I'd actually been there six weeks. I checked the calendar on my phone and realised he was correct. Everything was becoming a blur. Men would go home for their one week's leave but then seemed to reappear after what felt like only a couple of days.

I became less and less myself and agitation was there constantly! Men speaking to me whilst I was trying to eat, lazy overpaid Health & Safety Officers handing out safety leaflets with appalling grammar on them, listening to workmates talking about nonsense, Polish men working incredibly dangerously, labourers being given tradesmen's jobs, a safety seminar conducted by some southern ponce who talked to us all like children, having to repair foreigners work, the weather…

When I heard that one of the lads had received a bottle over his head in one of the pubs I realised that I was living in The Lord Of The Flies! This island seemed to be turning everyone feral!

I know that some men who work nightshift end up putting weight on, I go the opposite way, I *always* lose weight. Working continuously coupled with the fact that I was completely off the booze meant that I lost more weight than usual. I started that job weighing just shy of 14st and I left it weighing only 12.5st! When I looked in the mirror on my last day I didn't recognise the pale, skinny ghost of man who was staring back at me. I don't regret working that many shifts because it completely pulled me out of the shit but it's something that I hope I never have to do again!

Because I had been living on a camp with everything provided it meant that I had barely spent a penny. When I got home I felt like I'd had a little win on a scratch card. Feast or famine! The feeling of having money in the bank is even better than the feeling of shooting your muck all over a woman's face! But what was a man like me going to do with all that money?

P.S

I was only joking about fucking trees…honestly

CHAPTER SIX

FREEDOM OF SPEECH! IN A SOCIETY THAT FUCKING STINKS!

*"There is only one problem with Islam.
A lot of the men who practise it are
sister shagging thick cunts!"*

B.J Steel

1

On May 8th 2015 we got the results for the General Election. The news was bittersweet. Luckily Labour had been smashed to pieces but unfortunately the Tories were to rule supreme...I had hoped for a coalition. Overall though I breathed a sigh of relief when the Tories won. Before you hit the roof please allow me to explain myself. The generation of men above me absolutely hate the Tories with a burning passion. This hate comes from the actions of Maggie Thatcher in the 1980's, I can't say that I blame these men for their feelings.

As that older generation of men say "I will *never* vote Tory!" then me and hopefully the rest of my generation say "I will *never* vote Labour!" Firstly I should point out that I don't vote for either of these two parties, but if I had a gun put to my head and I was forced to vote for one of them, then I can tell you that the choice would be *very* easy. I would rather let Gary Glitter babysit my kids than vote for Labour!

Thatcher destroyed communities, Blair destroyed a country! Under Labour millions of immigrants flooded into an unprepared England, crippling the NHS, schools, welfare system and the housing market. Taxes shot up and apprenticeships were scrapped meaning foreign labour was the only way of filling skilled jobs. If Labour are for the working man then I'm a smelly gypo!

Tony Blair was a ruthless dictator! Under him unattainable targets were imposed upon every aspect of the public sector (except for the politicians themselves of course). After 9/11 he pumped his people full of unnecessary fear and then exploited that fear by robbing us of our civil liberties. He led his country to war when his country really didn't want to go. He had local councils spy on their inhabitants. Anyone who spoke out against his policies received derogatory labels. And finally of course we all live in a much more dangerous world now because of him and those two *evil* cunts Dick Cheney and Donald Rumsfeld.

They say that history repeats itself. When it comes to politics recent decades have proven that statement to be oh so true. This is what happens in the swings and roundabouts world of the two party politics. Labour comes into power and they've always got loads of money to spend. When the Conservatives finally regain power the country is absolutely fucked! This has been going on for decades. Doesn't that give a clear message dear reader?

Labour was a party set up by genuine socialists who wanted to help the working man and the original Labour government did just that. However corruption and greed gets the better of everyone. The modern

Labour party shows the same contempt towards the working man that the Conservatives always have. The only difference I can see between these two parties now is Labour loves high taxes and they refuse to even admit that we have an immigration problem!

2

Every single year in England we are guaranteed to have at least one news report talking about the lack of diversity in the top jobs.

Women have consistently proved the world over that they are just as capable as men. When it comes to politics women have proved that they can run countries BUT when women's numbers are increased in government it leads to one devastating consequence…political correctness gets out of hand and I fucking hate political correctness!

Men and women are very, very different. Let's step into a man's working environment and imagine a group of men sat chatting. If one of these men flippantly said the word 'wog' or 'Paki' none of the other men would bat an eyelid. The man who used the word won't be racist, he's either used it for comedic effect or it's just a word he's grown up with. In my opinion that man has done absolutely nothing wrong and at the end of the day all he's done is say a word.

So what?! If there had been a black person present at the time then that completely changes the situation. That man would now become a racist and also a bully and *that* is wrong.

Now let's step into a woman's working environment and imagine a group of women sat chatting. If one of these women used the word wog or Paki there would be a sharp intake of breath from all the other women in the room, followed by an awkward silence. Within an hour she would be called into the boss's office (after being stabbed in the back) and either be sacked or suspended! Welcome to the birth of political correctness!

Also women fucking *hate* each other! I really don't understand why this is. A woman will look at another woman and just see an enemy and a threat! I wonder how many women genuinely like their mother-in-law?

When it comes to ethnic diversity in jobs it's a subject that I find absolutely ludicrous! England is 85% white so of course that's going to be reflected in the workplace. If someone from an ethnic minority gets a job on merit then there's nothing wrong with that. If however they got the job purely because of the colour of their skin then that is a highly racist act and that will only breed racism!

When I was 24ish there was a newspaper report about a woman trying to get a job in the Environment Agency. She got told over the phone that she couldn't have an interview because she was white! She then went straight to the newspapers. In those days I hated my profession with a passion and I tried many times to get out of it. I know for a fact that this girl wasn't lying because I had also phoned the exact same company a few weeks earlier. I have a love for the outdoors and when I saw the Environment Agency advert it caught my eye. It was basically an apprenticeship scheme within the company and although the starting wages were low the job sounded interesting so I rang the number. At the bottom of the advert itself was this line,

'People from an ethnic minority are especially welcome'

When I rang the number the man quickly asked about my race and politely told me that I didn't stand a chance! I told him that it was wrong and left it at that. Me being a true Englishman I kept my moaning to myself. When I saw that newspaper article I was glad and also a little bit ashamed that I hadn't done anything about it myself. Dear reader, imagine if the advert had said,

'White people are particularly welcome'

There would have been an absolute uproar! But that's just how it was in the days of Tony Blair's reign.

So there you go dear reader, I have been a victim of racism and political correctness in my own country! I have a right to be angry!

3

I'm a man of average intelligence and economics definitely isn't one of my strong points, but I really don't understand what this recession is about. A load of make-believe money that only ever existed on a computer screen was suddenly deleted causing the markets to crash! Why couldn't they just type the make-believe number back in again? Am I being completely wrong and naïve here?

Just when we thought peoples standard of living couldn't be eroded any further along comes this recession and shows us we were wrong! It's been a perfect excuse for companies to make people's lives even harder. At the start of the recession the exploitation going on in certain British companies was fucking disgusting! There is a very large crane hire company in England that had its books brimming with more work than ever before in its history early on in the recession. However it didn't tell its employees this fact, instead it told its employees that hard times were ahead and wages needed to be cut to avoid mass payoffs! Then of course there was the explosion in zero-hour contracts! How are things like this allowed to happen in a unionised democracy?!

A lot of people got to have a taste of a contractor's lifestyle when all this first happened. Some people will have had their contracts terminated for the very first time in their lives and many of these people will also have had to face up to the prospect of moving to where the work was. Welcome to our world people.

One big thing that pisses me off about the recession is how a country can be in debt to itself. We are all told to have savings in the bank for any bad times or unforeseen expenses. When the government asks the Bank Of England for money to keep society running why the fuck should we have to pay it back? It's our money in the first place and it's there for things like a recession. Also the banks shouldn't have been *directly* bailed out, instead that money should have been given to the little people. We could all have paid off our mortgages, meaning the banks would have got their money back plus everyone's biggest debt would have been cleared so we could have carried on consuming, then all those businesses wouldn't have gone bust.

On paper that sounds ethical and a perfect solution doesn't it? That was never going to happen though dear reader, the last thing that any government wants is its people to be free from debt, it's what makes us all slaves to the money.

4

Money makes people and it destroys people... compulsive gambling is one way it can destroy people. I once used to drink with a lad who was a manager in a betting shop and he would tell me all about the characters in that place. Some of these people were the dregs of society!

He told me one bloke had been sat in the shop one day blind drunk. When he left, the seat he'd been sat on was soaked in piss! The next time he came in the manager had pulled him up,

"Did you piss yourself in here the other day?"
The man replied,

"You know how it is mate"
It seems that pissing in his trousers in public places must have been a regular occurrence...he must of thought it was something *everyone* did.

He also told me about a man who was divorced and would get to see his daughter for only one weekend every fortnight (which is just plain wrong by the way). How did this man spend this precious time with his daughter? In the bookies! Both days she would sit with him in the shop for four to five hours, filling her time by drawing pictures on betting slips whilst her father ignored her! That's a fucking disgrace!

This bookies was next door to a pub and one man would sit in the pub from opening time until last orders, frequently popping in throughout the day to put his bets on. He did this every day of every week! I asked the lad how this was possible, I earn half decent wages but I couldn't afford to do that. He told me that the man was an alcoholic and the government sees this as a disease, therefore he is given a drinking allowance on top of all his benefits! Where do I even begin with this dear reader? Firstly I don't know of any disease that is cured by giving a person more of it. We don't see Ebola victims being injected with Ebola! If a government is that fucking soft why can't they just give him £3 a day for a bottle of cider? Or better still give him absolutely fuck all and let the lazy bastard rot! The money they would save means they could bring back income based benefits for the normal people who keep this fucking country running!

The character I heard about who got on my nerves the most was a very old and very nice man. The lad was telling me he used to talk to this man every day and he was really pleasant. One day this little old man had come into the shop in a *rage*, apparently some tabloid newspaper had ran a story about doing away with the royal family. This lad said to the old man,

"I don't mind the Queen but I can't stand the rest of them. *None* of them should be getting tax payers money though."

The old man didn't give a reply to this, he just quietly put his bet on. After that he never went to this lad's window again, he'd always use a different person to put his bets on! I can honestly say that I'm really glad that generation of people have just about died out! I'm not going to go into an outburst about the royals here because I don't have time for that pack of lazy, spoilt cunts! But that old man knew this lad, he didn't know the royals. How could he get so defensive about people he had never met and at the same time sacrifice a relationship with someone who he knew?! It was that thick 'Hero Worship' mentality that kept the working classes an impoverished race for so many years.

5

Before this chapter descends into vile bad taste I feel the need to say something a bit more positive.

We are a very lucky bunch us Englishmen. We have been raised in a country where, apparently, freedom of expression and liberty are its core values. Most people on this planet would be willing to lose an eye to have some of the freedoms that we have. More often than not we take really basic liberties for granted.

If I so wished I could start a relationship with a black girl, possibly called Ebony or even a homosexual man, probably called Julian. (This is theoretical dear reader) I would be able to freely walk down the street hand in hand with either of these two people without fear of retaliation. I am very lucky to live in a country where I am able to do these things.

But there's a problem, we English are just too fucking nice! We hate to make a fuss about *anything* and this has led to our good nature being completely exploited. Exploited by foreign religions. We are lucky that Christianity is on the verge of extinction in this country but the same cannot be said for these foreign ones.

Could Julian and I or *even* Ebony and I walk hand in hand through a Muslim area or Orthodox Jewish area without fear of retaliation? I don't think we could. I don't even think I would feel as if I was still in England. If abuse was hurled at us and I complained to the police no doubt I would just be told to stay away from these areas. Is this freedom of expression? Or is this English liberty being robbed from us by foreign religions who seem to have more rights in the eyes of the law than what we do? We throw pensioners into prison for not paying their council tax yet Pakistani men seem to be allowed to rape underage English girls. Just for even saying that last line I can get into more trouble than the rapists themselves! What would happen if a group of white men raped a Pakistani girl? Mob justice probably.

We need to stop being so fucking nice! That's the most positive thing you are going to get from me!

6

It seems that in 2015 our friendly Muslim cousins were never out of our news programmes. When they weren't shooting people in Paris and Copenhagen, planning to bomb carnivals in Germany, drowning Christian migrants in the Mediterranean, massacring tourists, forcing kidnapped schoolgirls to slit men's throats and at the centre of England's biggest ever paedophile scandal, then they were burning people alive in cages and hacking people's heads off!

I remember after the Charlie Hebdo massacre the UK government sent out letters to Mosques telling them that they had to do more to help combat terrorism. There was a *white* left-wing outpouring in response to that letter. One of the left-wing wankers is a man who is never off our TV screens called Owen Jones. I've never met this man but I actually *hate* him! He's an ugly little cunt who has a face that looks like its chewing on a foreskin. His reaction to that letter was to compare it to the IRA saga in the 1970's, saying that we didn't send out letters to the Catholic Church. How he came up with this analogy is beyond me! It is a known *fact* that hate is being preached in some UK mosques and Islamic schools! Also Charlie Hebdo has attacked Christianity more than any other religion but it wasn't a group of backwards Christians who murdered them. The way that do-gooders ignore the truth really boils my piss! We all know one thing about these fucking left-wing hypocrites dear reader, deep down inside even they know that the planet would be a far better place if Islam didn't exist.

The French have got a lot more balls than us British, the fact that they outlawed the face veil proves it. That will *never* happen in soft touch Britain. Let's not beat around the bush here, this ridiculous head wear that Muslim women sport has got nothing to do with religion! Women who willingly wear hijabs do it because they can't be arsed brushing their hair and women who wear face veils are pig ugly! The poor Muslim women in the world who are forced to wear that crap must think these western Muslim's are fucking idiots!

There are even female British Muslims running off to join Isis now! I really cannot believe how thick some people can be! I recently watched a documentary about Isis on Channel 4 and it showed a woman being stoned to death. Her 'crime' was adultery and one of the men stoning her was her *own* father! As far as I'm concerned we should be paying for these idiots plane tickets, why would we want these warped wankers in our country? As soon as they're gone block their passports and leave them to their beloved Isis!

I understand that a lot of Muslims are decent, law abiding citizens but I also know that they completely look down upon our culture and they have a superiority complex over us. In Europe it's become impossible now for a non-Muslim person to look at a Muslim who is dressed in sheets and sporting a beard without an element of distrust. Even if we know that they probably don't pose us any threat, it's still hard to ignore the fact that to them we are nothing more than 'infidels'. It's come to the point now where we only have one sane option left and that is to get Islam out of Europe! Now I'm no tyrant so I believe in giving people a chance. Any Muslim who is willing to denounce their faith should be able to stay. But they should be forced to stand in our city and town centres and recite this line,

"Allah is a fictional character who is about as real as Steve Guttenberg's successful post-1980's career. And Muhammad was a smelly little bastard, who secretly loved pork *so* much that he was occasionally caught fucking pigs! "

Once they have recited that line they can go back to their normal lives. However the practising of Islam will be a criminal offence! Anyone who is caught doing it will receive 1000 public lashes and then be deported! See dear reader, I'm a fair man.

7

Unfortunately for me I had one of my very rare trips to a church not too long ago. It was one of those big family events that you can't say no to. There was a full mass at this event and as I stood there completely bored, listening to the congregation droning on, I struggled to believe that people still drag themselves to these monotonous affairs once a week. My spirits were lifted however when the congregation burst into one of those rarest of things...an up-tempo hymn! Now I wasn't happy because I liked the song, I was happy because since becoming an Atheist this song has become a symbol to me of just how stupid religious people can be! Religious people don't question *anything* about their faith, they just blindly follow it like sheep. It's this ignorance which has made our world such a dangerous place.

The hymn I'm referring to is called 'Follow Me.' I hope the majority of you readers remember it. This is a song about Jesus brainwashing his twelve disciples and like I've already said, it's quite an upbeat tune. I kept myself amused by watching the bible-bashers within the congregation singing this song. They all had big grins and smiles whilst singing it and some of them were even wiggling their chubby little hips in what seemed like pure ecstasy! Below is the chorus from this song.

> *"Follow me, follow me,*
> *Leave your homes and family,*
> *Leave your fishing nets and boats upon the shore,*
> *Leave the seed that you have sown,*
> *Leave the crops that you have grown,*
> *Leave the people you have known and follow me"*

Now dear reader, let's put this song into the context of the 21st century shall we? I want you to imagine one those women who were stood singing this song so orgasmically! After that mass she goes home to find her son sat on the doorstep. He has some devastating news,

"Mam, I've got something to tell you. I've met this bloke who's been telling me things. I can't say for certain but I'm pretty sure that he's the Messiah and he wants me to follow him around the country preaching the word to everyone. Anyway, to cut a long story short, I've just popped over to tell you that I've quit my job and you and Dad are never going to see me again. Do us a favour? Tell my wife and kids that I've left a nice flan in the oven for them. See ya!"

The first thing that woman is going to do is to try and have her son sectioned! In this day and age we call that sort of behaviour being part of a cult. The truth is ALL religions start out as a cult and then for some bizarre reason they manage to spread.

Christians are the biggest hypocrites on the planet! There's not one of them that actually practices the so called teachings of Jesus Christ and that's because those teachings go completely against human nature. These Christians leave church on a Sunday and then start work on a Monday where they turn into right devious bastards!

The most annoying thing is 99% of Christians haven't even read the bible and they don't seem to think that this is an issue! Their whole existence is based on a book that they haven't even bothered to read, that is the height of ignorance! Maybe one day they should sit down and read about how lovely people like Abraham and Moses really were. If people base their morals on figures like that then it would be better for the rest of us if they were fucking dead!

8

There's one word that those Christians absolutely hate…SEX. The mere mention of that disgusting word makes them want to vomit! I wonder why? After all it's as natural as breathing and eating and it's also the reason we are all here. What is it about SEX that makes those Christians blush so much? We non-Christian men love talking about sex and I know that women are no different.

I can remember having a bit of an argument with a man that I didn't like very much (he loved to gossip). This imbecile said that humans are dirtier now than ever before! I think he had come to this conclusion purely because of the amount of porn that exists today. I can remember saying to him,

"Do you know what Greek sex is?"
He replied "No", so it was confirmed that I was dealing with a complete mong.

"Greek sex means 'anal sex'. It comes from ancient Greece when people absolutely loved fucking each other's bumholes. Have you heard of ancient Rome?"

"Of course I have!"

"So you already know about the mass orgies? Slaves being forced to have sex with animals?"
Some people are ignorant, we haven't got dirtier at all, we have always been filthy! We are all nothing more than a species of animal and it's in the bedroom where our animalistic side comes out.

However SEX does make *everyone* feel uncomfortable in one way though…the thought of it being how we got here. We don't even like to see our parents kissing each other never mind fucking each other. Many of us will have been unlucky enough to walk in on our parents 'doing it'. It's quite a horrible moment isn't it? With this in mind I thought I might set myself a challenge. A challenge to see if I can make you, the dear reader, squirm in your fucking seat! For me to achieve this then you're going to have to play along and do everything I say.

I want you to picture your own mothers face. That wonderful person who has nurtured you since you were nothing more than a bean in her belly. Picture her face smiling, that loving mother who has fed you, clothed you, bathed you and read you bedtime stories. Isn't she smashing? As you picture that loving face you notice that she isn't smiling, she's grimacing! Why is she grimacing? As you take a step back in your mind to look at your mother you can now see the reason for the grimace. Her hair is being pulled right back by the man stood behind her. It's your father and he's absolutely bollock naked! As his little moob's bounce up and down you notice that he's pulling the most awful sex face that you have ever seen in your life! As he yanks your mothers head back and slaps her arse he starts to speak in a voice that you've never heard him use before, grunting the words,

"Go on take it!...Take it you fucking pig!"
Your mother is screaming out…
That, dear reader, was the moment you were conceived! The next time you go around your mams

house for your tea I want you to picture that moment as you kiss her on the cheek. Maybe even say to her,

"I was reading about you the other day"

9

Babies piss me off! Well, not the babies themselves but all the stupid advice that comes along with them. Both times that my ex-wife was pregnant we were given a list of do's and don'ts. It was ridiculous! Even the midwife told us that the list changes from year to year. We hear the generation above us say,

"We didn't do that when you were a baby"

When my generation turns into grandparents we are going to be saying exactly the same thing. But the thought of what the list will be like when I'm an old man is scary! DONT drink water whilst pregnant! DONT touch babies without wearing rubber gloves! DONT speak to the baby in a language in doesn't understand! In fact the way societies going it will become a criminal offence to break anything on the list. I can just imagine the chaos in our streets,

"Look!!! That pregnant woman is eating an egg! I have never seen *anything* so outrageous in my entire life! Phone the police!"

It's going to be absolutely mental!

As I'm typing these words, right now in some jungle in the world a baby is being born. It's being handled with muddy hands and its suckling on one of its mothers scabby tits. That baby is going to grow into a kid who is ten times fitter than the majority of kids in England. Its mother isn't reading some backwards list of do's and don'ts! In fact I'd love to see her reaction if she did see the list. I have no doubt that she would see us as a very stupid breed of people!

10

A big problem in this modern society is allowing our youth to have pipe dreams. Every kid in the west believes that they're going to be rich when they grow up and it was the same for me and everyone I know. Once we do grow up we realise that we aren't going to be rich but we spend our entire adult life clinging on to the hope of winning the lottery. (I can remember when I was married I was working a nightshift one night and my wife rang me up in a bit of a mood. We had one line each on the lottery that we put on every week religiously. This night she had checked the lottery numbers on teletext and to her delight she saw that we had all six numbers! For a moment she really believed that we'd won the jackpot, however upon closer inspection she realised she'd made a bit of a booboo. Three numbers were from my line and three numbers were from hers. A grand total winnings of

£20! I would rather have not won anything! Why she had bothered to ring me up at work with this dispiriting news is anyone's guess. Women can be fucking stupid!)

It seems that the parents of today help to fuel the pipe dreams of their kids. This will be something that I'm never going to do with my two. Right now somewhere in England there will be a little girl called Chantelle. It's Chantelle's destiny to grow up and clean toilets for a living. There is nothing wrong with being a toilet cleaner, it's a lot more important to our society than being a footballer. However little Chantelle will have a passable singing voice. Her parents will be quite thick and they will tell Chantelle that when she grows up she's going to be a singer and will probably win The X-Factor. Those parents have just destroyed that little girl's life. She won't grow up to be a singer and neither now will she ever become the toilet cleaner that she was destined to be. Because she has grown up with a delusion then cleaning toilets will be far too beneath her. Instead she will become part of the most recent entry to our class system…The Scrounging Class. Chantelle will knock out five or six kids and she'll delude the lot of them like her parents did to her. Instead of them getting real jobs that society needs they will also join The Scrounging Class.

So who becomes the toilet cleaners that these people should've been? The immigrants who come to our shores to do *any* job they can, just so that they can live in a country that the rest of us were lucky enough to be born in. How did it get like this? I'm pretty sure it's not what Clement Attlee had in mind when he created the welfare system.

The Scroungers Class needs to be scrapped and the scum who are part of it need to be forced into the jobs that they can't be arsed doing! We can't rely on thick parents to stop polluting their kid's minds, so now it should be the job of our teachers. They need to recognise the limitations of each kid in their class and then help the kids mentally prepare for the jobs that they are almost certainly guaranteed to end up in.

11

Education in our schools doesn't seem to be getting any better these days. When you look at the kids in China they are human calculators. English schools, rather than trying to teach our kids to be brilliant at mathematics like their Asian counterparts, are happier trying to drum political correctness into them.

In the novel 1984, the main characters job is to censor archived news stories so that they don't conflict with the current propaganda of the government. We can see this censoring of history in our own schools today. The single biggest part of British history is the British Empire. Our tiny little island managed to rule three quarters of the planet at one point. Our kids don't have a clue about this fact! Why you ask? Because we didn't rule the world by being nice…we did it by being ruthless and by being a little bit evil. So because we were a bit nasty we shouldn't teach our kids about it, better to just forget that it ever happened. This is the single biggest example of political correctness gone mad in our country right now. It is absolutely ABSURD! It's the equivalent of German kids not being taught about the two World Wars!

But the political correctness doesn't end there, schools are wasting valuable teaching time on trying to achieve the unachievable…they want to try and eradicate bullying. Now I hate bullies and it's any parent's worst thought to think of their own kids ever being bullied, but even I know that this is a complete waste of money and time! Kids are cruel, they always have been and they always will be. Schools need to accept it and put all their efforts into meaningful education.

They want to start teaching sex education to eight year olds now. Part of modern day sex education also includes talking about homosexuality. I can remember being eight vividly and all I was interested in was playing out, climbing trees and setting fire to things.

What eight year old needs to have deep discussions about cocks, vaginas and men's bumholes? (Actually I've got a confession to make. At the age of eight I would secretly flick through the lingerie pages in my mams catalogues… without really understanding what it was about those pictures that made me feel so happy.)

The truth is fat kids will always be picked on and boys who hang around with the girls will always be picked on and I can guarantee that that will *never* change. If schools are so obsessed about getting kids to act the complete reverse of human nature then there are better ways. Rather than wasting teaching time on it, they should just go direct to the parents. If a kid is obese ring the mother and tell her to stop feeding them so much, if a boy is a bit camp tell the mother to stop letting him bring dolls to school, if a kid turns up in half-mast trousers and a shirt that hasn't been washed in three weeks then ring the mother up and ask the scruffy cunt what the fuck she's playing at! If all these types of parents choose to ignore the teacher's advice then they're going to have to accept the fact that unfortunately their poor kids are going to be bullied every day.

12

Growing up isn't easy for anyone but this generation of kids growing up in England right now have my deepest sympathies and worries. Every part of society has now become solely about money, *'How much can we make? How much can we save?'* There will come a time in the future when even all our communal parks will have 'paid parking' car parks. When I think of what the future holds for my own kids it really scares me. The costs of housing, the cost of education, the cost of fucking everything! Trust me I'm under no illusion of who's actually going to have to pay for all these things!

When we grow up we are given very little guidance in life. Our schools aren't interested and our parents are too miserable in their own lives to be any help to their kids. I was really lucky in the fact that I grew up in a very loving household, but when it came to life guidance all my parents ever told me is,

"You can be *anything* you want to be"

At first glance that might seem like a very nice thing to tell a child but trust me from experience, I think it's a pretty stupid thing to say to a kid. Every human being has his/her own limitations, I was never going to be a brain surgeon or a rocket scientist. When I did enter the big bad world I was totally unprepared for it, I had expected the world to fall into my lap. I believe it's the duty of every parent to sit their kids down at the age of 16 and say,

"Listen, the next ten years are going to be the hardest years of your life. You are going to have to try really hard in life and you're going to have to do a lot of things that you really don't want to do… but that's just part of becoming an adult. But don't worry because life will get easier the older you get."

It's that last line that's the most important, we don't want to drive our kids to suicide so you need to dangle a carrot. But it is also the truth, life has gotten easier for me. When my kids were born going to work didn't bother me anymore. I had to provide for two helpless little babies who were completely dependent on me…also it was nice to get away from the loud little bastards!

If any young men are reading this now and you feel angry or disillusioned then trust me, life does get easier. One day you will realise that this industry we've been thrown into can offer you a good life, but you have to be willing to grab it. There's one thing I don't do now since I've hit my thirties and that's wish my life away. Even when times are unpleasant I prefer to just see my way through them, rather than wish another chunk of my short existence down the drain

13

Every government in the world, be it democratic or authoritarian, have one simple thing in common…they fucking hate pensioners! Of course our greedy, fat politicians want themselves and their families to live for as long as possible and they will use our taxes to feather their own nests and have an extremely comfortable and care free retirement. However when it comes to the rest of us they really can't understand why we don't just die the day we stop being any use to society! They would prefer for us to be six feet under as soon as we hit our expiry date and then let our relatives squander our life savings on things that really have no importance in life.

Because of modern medicine we are all living longer and so the government tells us we should expect to have to work longer. I have one big problem with this argument. A seventy year old is still a fucking seventy year old! When I'm seventy, I'm not going to be any fitter than a seventy year old who is walking around today! I'm going to be just as fucked as he is, regardless of what medicines they invent! There are jobs and conditions in my own industry that we should *never* expect an old man to work in. These are jobs that no politician would ever put up with in their youth, never mind their golden years.

When my generation is retired the state pension will have been scrapped…a luxury only reserved for the Scrounging Class. When all our money is gone we'll be expected to sell everything we own and move into an expensive care home where we can expect to be mistreated by untrained staff on a daily basis. That money from our house's and possessions should have gone to our kids (who couldn't be arsed caring for us themselves because they've got too many of their own problems).

Old people's homes are an invention of the western capitalist society. People from every other society in the world really can't understand why we throw our parents away out of sight and out of mind! It's pretty fucking barbaric when you sit and think about it.

I've always imagined that being in an old people's home would be like being back at school. No one really wants to be there, splitting into different groups, gossiping and taking the piss out of each other. Of course you'd be trying to get your fingers sticky with some of the ladies as well.

I don't really think I'd be suited to a care home. When I reach the stage when I know my marbles are starting to go and my knob is getting a bit too limp, I'm going to go on the biggest bender of my life and then afterwards jump straight on a plane to Switzerland where I can go out with some dignity. (Maybe by then in England humans will have the same rights as their pets!)

After I'm dead people can do whatever they want with my corpse! Fuck it or shit on it…I'm not going to know anything about it!

CHAPTER SEVEN

I'VE GOT A SERIOUS PROBLEM

1

I've got a serious problem in life dear reader…it's myself! I am my own worst enemy! Once the seed of an idea is planted in my stupid little brain it can't be stopped from growing. The trouble is, I've never had a good idea in my entire life!

After nearly five months of unemployment followed by working 56 shifts on the belt I told myself that I deserved a treat. But there can only be one treat for me and I know that you have already guessed what it is. I have a very addictive personality (the fact that I've released three books in the space of a year proves that) and it just so happens that I've discovered the most addictive place on Earth. I tell myself that a Thailand addiction is a good one to have. Who wouldn't want long frequent holidays there? But it's also a very expensive addiction and at this point in my life I should be putting other priorities first. But I just can't help myself!

When I returned home from that job the logical thing to have done would have been to find another job and then carry on getting my house finished. But to me having money in the bank and *not* going to Thailand is the equivalent of a smoker walking around with a packet of fags in his pocket and *not* smoking them. Or a gambler walking into a bookies with £50 in his hand and *not* putting a bet on. Or a Health & Safety Officer walking past a group of working men and *not* sticking his fucking nose in! In other words…impossible!

When it comes to booking my holidays I will always have a devil on one shoulder and an angel on the other. The angel will give me two or three solid reasons why I shouldn't be going away but the devil will give me ten superficial reasons why I should. The argument that won me over this time was this, '*Half the year has already gone in what seems like an instant! 4 months wasted on the dole followed by 2 straight months of 'hard' graft! Even a starving child in Africa would tell me that I deserve a holiday!*'

And so it was to be, yet again the Devil won. After having two weeks off at home with my kids, I set off on my sixth holiday to Pattaya in the space of 29 months.

I do have plans to see a lot more of this planet but those holidays require months of planning with a travel companion. Pattaya is a place where I know I can just turn up on my own whenever I'm able to.

This would turn out to be a completely different holiday from the previous one, but I already knew that it would be before I'd even set off. Whereas that last holiday had been about shagging all the stress out of my system, this holiday was about pure relaxation. However there is a very fine line between relaxation and complete bone idleness! I had emailed Greg to let him know I was returning but unfortunately for him he was experiencing financial difficulties at home. I'd suggested to him that he should just take out a bank loan and then at the end of the holiday he could throw himself off his balcony. It was a generous suggestion which he declined.

I booked it properly this time, I stretched my 30 day visa to breaking point. I was actually returning home in the early hours of my 31st day but as long as I passed through immigration before midnight it wouldn't matter.

After that girls comments about everyone knowing me on Soi's 7 and 8 I had told myself at the time that I should probably stop in a different part of the city when I returned. However when it came to booking up though I said fuck it and stuck to what I knew. I said to myself, *'Hopefully there's been mass payoffs on Soi's 7 and 8...a big turnaround in the workforce!'* I actually booked the same hotel from my second trip which I know will surprise some of you reading this. It was on Soi 7, a road I had vowed not to stay on again, but the allure of a dirt cheap sea-view room was too much for me to say no to. Although this holiday would turn out to be peppered with bad luck from start to finish, I still really enjoyed it.

On the flight to Dubai I witnessed a Muslim man aggressively shouting at his wife. She was dressed from head to toe in a black death shroud! I felt three emotions when I saw this, pity for the woman, anger towards the man but also deep, deep joy! *'This is fucking perfect for my book!'* Sat with them was a young boy and young girl, both the kids and the man were wearing western clothes. I felt truly sorry for those children. Judging from the man's mannerisms I was 99% sure that he was a wife beater, it's more than likely that the little boy will grow up to be exactly the same. As for the little girl, I wondered how long it would take before she was given her very own death shroud to wear. Two innocent little human beings who were destined to be corrupted by a backwards religion in a backwards culture.

My arrival in Pattaya was met with my usual emotions, a buzz of excitement and also now a feeling that I'm returning home. That first night I discovered that the job cuts on Soi's 7 and 8 had been deeper than what I had first hoped for! Three of my favourite women had moved on, one to some other part of the city and two to better lives abroad. I couldn't begrudge that.

I know that the majority of men who've read my first book will already have been to Thailand but I've got a feeling that many of you reading this won't have had that pleasure. To those of you who haven't been I want to promise you now that there is *no* better way to start your day than laying in your hotel bed, receiving an hour long massage and then getting a good piping off at the end of it. Its pure bliss.

When I woke up on my second day I decided that I wanted this treat. The procedure is really simple, you lay in your bed, lazily reach for the bedside phone, call reception and tell them that you require a massage. Twenty minutes later a woman will be knocking on your door.

A Thai massage can range from soothing to borderline painful and I believe that the woman who turned up to my room on this day was a man hater. She absolutely brutalised me! The moment she started she was digging her thumbs right into me. My male pride prevented me from asking her to be gentler and I think my silence encouraged her to make it hurt just a little bit more. At one point she was walking up and down on my back. There is nothing unusual about this technique but normally the woman will try to spread her weight, this bully was sticking her toes into my back! When she completed this hour of torture she didn't even offer me a happy ending! The thought of a blowjob was the only thing that had gotten me through it, she might as well have just slapped me in the face! When she left the room I felt used, abused and also very cheap. As I laid there masturbating I had to stop myself from sobbing.

That second day would turn out to be quite a cursed day for me as it was filled with unfortunate events. The next bit of bad luck would turn out to be complete public humiliation.

I *did* have a favourite bar in Pattaya, I'd popped in there on my first night to have one drink and say hello to everyone. When I turned up there on my second night there was a bargirl there who knew me from a previous trip and she was privy to some very sensitive information about me. Basically she knew that I'd fucked ladyboy's. This is something that you never want the women to know because it can be like receiving the kiss of death.

Within two minutes of me sitting down the gossip had spread around the bar like wildfire and a couple of the girls came up and confronted me about it. This was gentle banter that I could take on the chin but then the gossip spread to the band. In a moment of sheer female bitterness the lead singer used her microphone to loudly question my sexuality. Everyone at that bar and the surrounding bars were staring at me. My constant and also feeble attempts to sit at a bar looking both cool and mysterious had been destroyed! On the outside I laughed and just shrugged it off, but on the inside I felt like jumping up onto the stage and raping her mouth! After that night I never went back there. (It's a little bit ironic that this would turn out to be my first ever holiday in Pattaya where I didn't have a ladyboy. I'm not saying I'm converted or anything but fucking another man is a bit like fucking the exhaust pipe of a car…you really have to be in the right mood)

This night would turn out to be one of my 'indecisive' nights. This where I go from bar to bar telling myself I'll see a more attractive lady in the next place. This will happen all night long until suddenly its daylight, I'm pissed out of my skull and the pickings are slim. These ingredients have led me to sleeping with some of Pattaya's 'less desirable' women. Whenever this happens I tell myself that I'm merely committing an act of kindness, but that's just complete and utter bollocks!

When it got to the end of my second night I ended up picking an older woman. She was wearing a little dress, she was skinny and the skin on her arms and legs was nice and tight. When I got her back to my room I realised I had been duped by some *very* false advertising! Everything under that dress had sagged, including her arse. If I could have taken legal action at that point in time then I would've done. It would have been cruel of me to ask her to leave and I'm not a cruel person, so in a moment of pure selflessness I had sex with her.

I mounted her from behind realising she must have been even older than what her face had first led me to believe. With this realisation came a thought, *'My knob is in a place that thousands of its cousins must have been in before it'* I did my best to push that thought from my mind. I'm generally a silent cummer but when I reached the point of climax with her I let out a groan of relief! When I awoke later on she was still asleep so I took a look under the covers. She didn't look too dissimilar to a corpse. Maybe I am a pervert after all?

After fucking her again she left my room so I took a stroll to the beach and found that it was really quiet. Due to Russia's collapsed economy it meant all those miserable bastards were gone, obviously this was a brilliant thing but still, I never mind perving on those beautiful moody Russian women in their thongs on the beach. I sat there listening to my iPod and supping on a Singha, then Svefn-g-Englar came on in my headphones. I cranked the volume right up. As I sat watching the sun glistening off the waves, the song was giving me shivers right down to my toes. It was possibly the most relaxed that I have ever felt in my life…a little moment that I will never forget. That moment rekindled my love for the beach but unfortunately I didn't get to visit as much as I would've liked due to Pattaya being shrouded in cloud for the vast majority of the holiday. Sunshine became as rare as a generous Jew.

2

On my third night I found out that a girl I knew had died, she had only been 30 years old. Shortly after discovering this I was sat at one of my regular bars feeling a little bit depressed. A woman I had met on my third holiday worked at this bar and on most nights of my trips I will have a chat with her and buy her a drink. After two minutes of sitting next to me she said,

"I not sit with you if you no fun"

This was another Pattaya eye opener for me. An English woman deep down wouldn't really give a shit about the death of a stranger either but at least she would've spent a few minutes pretending that she did before trying to lighten the mood. In some places life is too cheap.

I have no illusions when it comes to Pattaya, at its core it's a really horrible place and it's impossible not to feel sorry for the women who work there. But it's just such a brilliant place for men! We all become working class versions of Hugh Hefner in our short time there. I have my own little motto for that city, *'Heaven for men...Hell for women'* Any other men who have already thought of this line in the past, then be rest assured that it has now been copyrighted by me. Just check the back of page one (more commonly referred to as page two).

It may surprise you to learn that I have a long list of annoyances in life dear reader and Pattaya has its very own list. One of my lesser annoyances is some women's obsession with my nose. I am frequently accused of having a 'silicone nose' and to prove to these women that they're talking out of their bulletholes I have to let them aggressively pinch it. The reason for this minor obsession is because the Thais don't have a very pronounced bridge to their noses. This has led some western men to say cruel things like, *'They look like they've been hit in the face with a frying pan'* or more simply *'pan-faced'*. I don't think these men have seen how beautiful some of these women are. (Although even I have to admit that some of the less attractive women do have faces as flat as an A4 piece of paper) This has led a lot of Thais to getting nose jobs, especially the ladyboy's. I really hate the women getting this operation. A few times now I have seen some stunning women with nose jobs and my initial thoughts upon seeing them were that they were ladyboy's. For me personally this means I could never be seen in public with them, just in case other people were thinking the same thing.

Thais also have an obsession with white skin, because in that country it's a sign of wealth. When you see the Thais who work in television their skin is even milkier than ours. In the west we have tanning creams and tanned celebrities and in the east they have whitening creams and white celebrities. Again this is something that I don't like, the darker the skin the better, in my own pointless opinion.

I had written in my first book that Thai women have a sense of humour similar to that of a western child and I have a perfect example from this holiday. I was sat with a girl one night who was teaching me some new words and she told me that the Thai word for pork is 'moo'. I told her at the time that this didn't make sense as moo was the international sound of a cow. She didn't really understand what I was trying to say so I had to do an impression of a cow for her. When I did this she burst into a fit of hysterics, this was a 25 year old woman! I have a young daughter and I can say with pride that I have taught her the art of 'piss-taking'. If I had done this impression for her she would've simply shook her head at me and called me an "Idiot". I might have taught her too well because these days I'm too scared to try and put her down in case she humiliates me. I feel really sorry for that little boy out there somewhere in the world who will one day marry her.

I'm a great believer in eating the local food of a country that you are holidaying in (and also of learning the basic pleasantries of the language) but on this holiday my hotels close proximity to the Pig & Whistle Pub meant I was guilty of having quite a few English breakfasts this trip. I feel no shame, there is no better meal when you're feeling rough.

I was sat in that pub one day, having my very late breakfast, and there was a Scottish pensioner and his Thai wife sitting on the table next to me. They sat in silence as he read his British newspaper. Every now and again he would have a little outburst over the things he was reading about, cost of living, politics etc. His wife would ignore every word that he was saying. I can remember thinking to myself, '*My God, I hope I don't turn into him one day*' and then moments later came another thought, '*Actually I'm probably already halfway there!*'

I had one of those perfect Pattaya nights out in my second week. Early on in the night I had won every game of pool that I'd played, then I went on a gogo bar crawl and each club became filthier than the last. Then I ventured into a Ping-Pong show where I became a very willing guinea pig for the experiments up on the stage. After that I went to Club Insomnia where I was made to feel like a god! This being one of my indecisive nights I left the club alone and headed back to Soi 7, jumping onto a tuktuk along the way. Enroute the tuktuk picked up three large, loud drunken men who I assumed were all Yanks. I got talking to one of them and he told me that he was Canadian. When I'm tipsy I can be guilty of having a slightly cheeky sense of humour and when he told me this I asked him,

"So you're a moose fucker then?"
This is the fourth time that I've said this to a Canadian and it's also the fourth time that question has been met with a stony glare. I'm starting to believe that Canada is a nation of boring cunts! Luckily his two mates started laughing and one of them said to me,

"I'm Hawaiian, so what does that make me?"
I have to admit dear reader, this completely flummoxed me, I know absolutely nothing about Hawaii. He broke the awkward silence by saying,

"You're English aint yer? That makes you a sheep shagger!"

I had nothing but respect for this man, he clearly had some knowledge of my country and most Yanks don't even realise that I'm English when they first speak to me. Then the last man piped up,

"I'm an American, so what does that make me?"

By now the tuktuk had pulled into my stop and the driver was waiting for me to get off. Pressured by time I had no option but to say the first thing that popped into my head,

"You're an Iraqi fucker"

This comment was met with whoops of joy and cheesy high fives were given all round. I remember walking away from them feeling quite pleased with myself. As I walked down the street with my head held high I spotted a woman and bar-fined her. It had been a perfect night and it deserved a perfect ending, unfortunately it didn't get one...

I have been cursed in life dear reader, very fucking cursed! For some bizarre reason women always assume that I've got a big dick and the painful truth is...I just don't! I'm not just talking about Thai women here, a couple of drunken English women have said to me in the past,

"I bet you've got a big cock"

I really don't know why this assumption is made, if I was a big burly bloke maybe I'd understand it but I'm not, I stand at 5'11" and I'm average build. When I do get a woman back to my room and get my little tiddle out I can expect one of two reactions, either a pair of squinting eyes or a sigh of disappointment. Why is it that women look at us and try to gauge the size of our manhood's? To them we are nothing more than pieces of meat...sex objects! Imagine how women would feel if we men looked at them in the same way?!

So on this perfect night I had taken a woman back to my room and when I exposed myself she let out a little giggle and asked me,

"Why you small?"

Admittedly her giggle was quite infectious and I found myself sniggering like a stupid fool. When I nailed her I attempted to use my full six inch length to try and punish her! But to be honest it might as well have been floating motionless in the centre of big bucket. Those words are going to haunt me for the rest of my life.

3

Every time I go to Pattaya I always like to have at least one African woman (or 'darkie' to the less sophisticated reader). Usually they're from Uganda and I've found that they're always quite well educated. I will normally spend a good few hours chatting with them before completely exploiting them. The African I had this holiday was from Botswana and she turned out to be incredibly naïve and also extremely racist.

We were sat drinking on my balcony and she told me that she absolutely hated Thai people. She said they were all evil and if you let one of them touch you then you receive bad luck. Obviously I told her she was talking bollocks and in the back of my head I was thinking, '*People like her are flooding into my country every single day and yet I'm the one who gets labelled a racist just for saying we have too many of them*'

I know it's wrong to laugh at people from poor countries but I have to tell you something that she said to me. The topic of religion popped up and I told her that I didn't believe in God. She said,

"Of course there is a God. If there is no God then why don't cockroaches come into our mouths whilst we sleep? He is protecting us."

Maybe this was a bit nasty of me but I laughed in her face and told her that was the stupidest thing I'd ever heard in my life. I then asked her where God was when six month old babies were getting their skulls smashed in by rifle butts.

What she lacked in education she made up for in life experience and we ended up chatting until the sun came up. At one point in the conversation she said to me,

"Men and women are as bad as each other. Men use women for sex and women use men for money" It's a cold hearted and often true view of the world which I already understand, but it was nice to hear it coming from a woman's mouth.

The next story I have to tell you is a little bit disgusting and any readers with sensitive tummies are advised to skip the next three paragraphs.

Dear reader, I absolutely love having my bumhole licked! There is no better feeling than another person's mouth greedily eating away on your rectum. It's wonderful. However, every time I go to Pattaya nowadays I always seem to get the 'shits'. When the shitting starts then the rimming HAS to stop, otherwise it's a recipe for disaster.

On this sixth holiday I stuck to my routine of getting the shits but this time it was worse than ever. I'm the type of man who believes in sweating an illness out of yourself but this time it was different. The sheer amount of uncontrollable, mucky brown bum water pouring out of my anus, coupled with the copious amounts of dehydrating alcohol I was drinking, was setting me on a path to serious problems. I had no option but to seek the help of a pharmacist. When I had walked into the shop I'd breathed a sigh of relief when I saw that it was a man working there. He sold me a course of pills which I immediately took up to my room and started. The effect was almost instant, I spent the next three days constipated. Given the choice of having bloated guts or sitting at a bar in fear of shitting myself then the answer was easy. I was able to go out, much like a woman wearing a discreet panty-liner...body confident. In every future trip I have I'll be visiting a pharmacy as soon as the shitting starts and I advise everyone else to do the same.

However before my trip to the pharmacy there was one night when I was lucky/unlucky in picking up a really filthy woman. When I was laid on my bed getting piped off she had started to lift my legs up. I knew at the time that I should have forced her hands back down but this was the first time that a Thai woman had ever pre-empted this exotic indulgence, so I stupidly let her carry on lifting them. When she made the journey south and put her tongue in there she removed it after a matter of seconds. I was to quickly find out the reason for her sudden loss of rectal appetite. The dirty fucking pig came straight up and shoved her tongue down the back of my throat and I was to finally discover what my own faeces tasted like! This was an experience I had hoped to avoid having...if not at least for a few more years. I went straight to the bathroom and washed my mouth out with mouthwash and she did the same. The sex that followed was carried out in an atmosphere of mistrust. This is one mistake that I will *never* make twice. If your shit tastes as bad as mine then I feel sorry for you.

The frequent bad luck this holiday reached its pinnacle just after the halfway point. There are some lessons in life that we learn the hard way, but sometimes a bit of common sense should have prevented us from ever having to learn them in the first place.

I picked up a woman from Walking Street one night and she was just my type, short and skinny. After I had finished making sweet, sweet love to her she had told me that she wanted to do something nice for me. As I laid there waiting to go to sleep she had taken a Vicks inhaler out of her bag. She opened it up and rubbed the contents onto her fingers, she then proceeded to rub these fingers on my temples and all over my forehead. Apparently this would have a soothing effect that would help me sleep, but the problem is I sleep on my front with my face buried into the pillow.

When I was to awake later that day to go for a piss I noticed in the mirror that my eyes were completely bloodshot. They were even redder than a used tampon. As the evening carried on they were becoming even more bloodshot. I was disgusted in their appearance so I stopped in that night in the hope of sleeping them back to normal. The next day they were even worse, as well as being red my eyelids had also puffed up. I had no option but to go back to the pharmacy. This time when I went in some young buck was sitting there and he recommended some eye drops. I took them to my room and administered them straight away. The moment I put them in, my eyes started stinging and alarm bells started to ring. Because I had already paid for and opened them, I carried on using them for a further 48 hours, this would turn out to be even stupider than letting that woman do that to me in first place! It was impossible for me to stop in two nights in a row, so I went out that night looking like a complete psychopath.

After two days of using these drops my eyelids were as swollen as Barack Obama's lips. When I looked in the mirror this day what I was staring at looked like pure evil! (I looked nearly as mental as one of those deaf people you see in the corner of our television screens) I returned to the pharmacy and luckily this time it was the man who had saved my bottom working there. He sold me some completely different drops and told me that I should not have been using the other ones. That night I had no option but to stay in again.

After four days of using the new drops one eye had gotten a lot better but the other eye was worse. The swelling had gone down but a thick visible film had grown over it and my vision had become cloudy. I went back to the pharmacy already knowing what he was going to say to me. He took one look at my eye and told me to go straight to the hospital. Going to hospital is something none of us ever want to do, especially when we're on holiday, but I had no choice. So with a heavy heart and a gammy eyeball I made my way to see a doctor.

I was prescribed two lots of drops and also a gel to use before sleep. This visit cost me £30 plus the money I'd already spent in the pharmacy totalled it to £40. Some of you may scoff at such cheap medical bills but let me put this into perspective for you. That's a potential four blowjobs! Maybe now you'll understand my agony?

By the time my eyes were completely back to normal (albeit with slightly blurry vision) I only had three nights of my holiday left! Eleven days marred by the stupid actions of an idiotic buffoon and my own vanity. We can all learn lessons from this story dear readers, the main one of them all is this. If a woman ever says to you,

"I want to do something nice for you."
Then be afraid…be *very* afraid!

4

During my time of having poorly eyeballs I had found that my penchant for hotel room massages had gone into overdrive. When you order a massage you are always asked if you want a Thai or oil massage. I don't know the reason why but I have *always* ordered the Thai. On this holiday, for the first time ever, I ordered an oil massage one afternoon. All I can say is what a difference!

When the woman came to my room I went and laid on the bed on my belly, wearing only some boxer shorts. She immediately took them off leaving me bollock naked. As soon as she started rubbing the oil in I questioned why I had never had one of these before. When she started massaging my arse she was pulling my cheeks wide apart and I remember thinking, *'I hope it's clean in there'.* After she finished doing that side of me she asked me to roll over, so I obliged. I assumed that she was going to cover me with a towel to give me a little bit of dignity but she didn't and I laid there feeling very vulnerable. (I had a flashback to being laid on the operating table when I had gotten the snip)

She immediately started massaging one of my thighs and she was making some pretty heavy contact with my willy and ballsack. I've had countless Thai massages and I've never once got a hardon during them, my best friend is quite well behaved when there is no physical contact. As soon as this woman's hands touched him he stood up to attention. At this point she started asking me where I was from and how long I was on holiday for. I answered and then asked her where she was from in Thailand. We were making small talk, both trying to ignore my little stiffy. For a moment it was quite embarrassing but then I thought to myself, '*Who gives a fuck?*' After that I started to enjoy it, praying for just a little more contact with him.

In the past all my happy endings have been blowjobs and sometimes sex, but this time I received an oily wank. Whenever a woman wanks me off she has one spare hand and usually a few spare fingers as well. This lady was using her spare hand to massage my balls and arse crack, I can remember watching her and thinking that she looked like a Thai version of my ex-mother-in-law. I grudgingly accept that that witch is an attractive woman but when I noticed this I thought it'd be better if I just shut my eyes. In the end I completely exploded all over my stomach. Although me and the lady were both impressed by the sheer amount of filth I had produced, I couldn't help feeling a pang of regret that I hadn't been able to perform so well on that black woman's face. This was undoubtedly the best massage I've ever had. Every time I rang for one after that, I always ordered oil and I stopped putting boxer shorts on.

A good book wouldn't be complete without a good love story. Fortunately for you and me, this isn't a good book and I'm not a fucking idiot, so don't be getting worried.

As I stated earlier, by the time the swelling and redness had completely disappeared from my eyes I only had three nights left. When I'd went out the first of these nights I told myself that I deserved a treat. Although I'd still really enjoyed this holiday it was a bit hard for me to ignore the many misfortunes I'd encountered. My treat would turn out to be something I'd never had before, a 'higher class' gogo girl.

I went out that night and got smashed and when the time was right I ventured into one of these classier establishments. When you go in these places every single woman looks like a model. In the place I had chosen one woman somehow managed to stand out from the rest. She was small even for a Thai, she can't have been any taller than 5' and she didn't have a single ounce of fat on her body, even Posh Spice would be jealous of her! She was on the stage dancing with everything she had and when she finished she came and sat next to me.

It's common for Thai women to look ten years younger than what they really are and this should be something that I've gotten used to by now, however I was still shocked to learn that she was only two years younger than me. Luckily she'd never had kids so she'd managed to maintain the tightest body that I have ever seen in my life. If God existed I would've thanked him there and then for creating such a perfect specimen. (Any men reading this who don't like skinny women would no doubt find her repulsive)

After a couple of minutes of chatting the conversation moved onto bar-fining. She asked me if I wanted short time or long time. I told her long time. She said her price was 3000 baht (roughly £60) and I told her,

"No chance."

She had a quick look at her watch and then dropped her price to 2000 baht. I agreed and then found out that the bar-fine was 1000 baht! This is the most I've ever paid in Thailand but I knew it was still a bit of a bargain for a woman of her calibre.

The sex with her was absolutely dynamite! At one point she was riding me in some weird position (that I can't be bothered trying to explain to you) and I put my hand on her stomach. It was as hard as rock! The next day she turned out to be one of those women who doesn't seem to want to leave the room. This wasn't a problem for me at all and I fucked her another three times that day. Normally I would be far too lazy to do this but the mix of her price plus the fact that I got a chubby on every time that I looked at her, meant I was able to muster up the extra energy.

As the afternoon grew later she told me that she had to go to work soon. I didn't say anything. She repeated this line a handful of times over the next couple of hours but I never made any reply. The truth is I would've been happy to spend the short remainder of my stay with her but her price wasn't very agreeable. When she looked at her watch and told me that she was already late for work I had to be honest and tell her that she was too expensive for me. In my head I'd hoped she would drop her price even more but when she told me that she can earn 2000 baht for short time I knew all hope was lost. When she got up and started cleaning my room completely naked it was a real struggle for me to keep my mingebag head on.

Although I'd found her personality to be mildly annoying I was still a bit devastated when she left my room. Shortly after I was stood at an ATM due to my dwindling funds and I found myself withdrawing more money than what I actually needed. Subconsciously I knew the reason why.

I went out that night and every bar took me one bar closer to hers. In the end I was sat in her bar and for the first time ever in that city I had a moment of self-doubt. She still had plenty of her shift left to go and she already knew that I was a bit of a mingebag...it was possible that she might knock me back! When she came and sat next to me I immediately asked if I could barfine her. She said yes with a big grin. She should never have shown me that grin dear reader, it meant she was getting the reduced rate without me even asking for it.

I took her out to a few nightclubs and she was wearing little white hot pants that didn't leave much to the imagination. Everywhere we went every man and woman stared at her. She was a stunner and nobody knew it more than her. What a fucking ego! Although she was only with me for a fee, it was still nice to know that I would be the only man allowed to fuck her that night.

My final nights in Pattaya are never good, no matter how hard I try to enjoy them. By this point of the holiday my body is always in pieces and I feel like I've shortened my life by one year, but even still, I always want to stay. On this final night she never bothered going to work (saving me paying the barfine). She started drinking the same time as me and by the time she was drunk she was getting on my nerves. I wasn't in the mood anyway but the mixture of her ego and also her very jealous attitude was grinding on me. Whereas every drink I had seemed to make me more sober, every drink she had made her just a little bit more annoying.

At one point we were in a gogo bar, she'd just been to the toilet and when she sat down she said to me,

"I just see my friend from Germany, I haven't seen him in long years. I told him we would go talk to him."

My response,

"Are you taking the piss? Why would I want to go and speak to some bloke? Go and speak to him on your own."

I was hoping she would as I'd been receiving some attention whilst she was away. Maybe this was the reason she said,

"No it's OK. I not leave you on your own."

By 01:00 she was staggering all over the place. I had to prop her up, walk her to the end of Walking Street and then back to the halfway point, making her drink two bottles of water along the way. It was embarrassing, not so much because of her but because of the looks people were giving me. I don't think acts of kindness are very well known on that street because those dirty glances seemed to suggest I was guilty of giving her a date rape drug. In the end I took her back to my room and put her to bed. I ate the food I'd picked up enroute and then passed out. What a shit night!

She stayed with me until my taxi picked me up at 21:00. Just before I left she spoke some nonsense and wrote her number down for me. This was discreetly lost whilst she wasn't looking. I've learnt the hard way to never swap contact details with these women.

In a *very* small way I regret bar-fining her. I know it's going to be a struggle for me to stay away from those expensive girls, now that I've gotten a taste for them. I already spend a *lot* of money in Thailand and the only way I could afford these women every night would be to either shorten my holiday, give up massages, severely reduce my drinking or try to get a very large wage rise. None of those things are going to happen!

When I got home the first two days were pretty bad and then I managed to pick myself up. Men who've never been to that city simply cannot comprehend how addictive it is. Leaving there is like having a massive comedown off the best drug you've ever taken. I met a man a couple of years older than me in 2015 whose life was the reverse of mine. He'd discovered Pattaya in his early twenties whilst he was still single, but then settled down afterwards, whereas I discovered the place after my divorce. He was telling me that he still thinks about that city frequently. Once it's under your skin I think it's there forever.

Pattaya is a double-edged sword for me. During chapter five I had turned 34, meaning I'm now in my mid-thirties. I don't have the stomach nor the stamina from my early twenties, sometimes now I'm forced into getting my eyebrows trimmed in the barbers and I can also be guilty of letting out a little groan whilst getting up from a really comfy chair, but even still, right now I feel like I'm in the prime of my life. It's Pattaya that makes me feel this way. The flipside is I don't want my thirties to end and for the first time *ever,* I'm now starting to worry about getting older. This is also down to Pattaya. Maybe one day I'll read that last bit back and chuckle to myself.

CHAPTER EIGHT

THE HOUSE THAT JACK BUILT

Dear reader, I've been really lucky in the fact that I've been gifted with a 'little dose' of Asperger's. One of its side effects is blunt honesty with people, this has got me into trouble in my private and work life many, many times. I wouldn't change it for the world. Because I am fully aware of my own mental issues it means I will always look for other peoples. I can spot another person's weakness quicker than a Jew can spot a coin on the pavement. I've come to realise that the most weak-minded people in life are always extreme extroverts. Their charisma is a façade used to try and hide some deep rooted problems. These people always seem to get the best jobs in life, which is why our planet is absolutely fucked!

I see my 'condition' as a virtue as I don't seem to get affected by things that would probably affect your average man. There are some men in the world who find it impossible to sit in a room on their own and there are other men who simply can't handle being single. I'm not one of them.

After the breakdown of my marriage I had to live in a rented flat for a year. It's not a year that I look back upon with any great fondness. There was only one good thing about that flat and that was the lovely view of the 1100 year old church from the front window. It just so happens that this was the church I got married in! I would imagine that any *normal* man would have sobbed every day at the sight of that view but not me. It was pleasant and I appreciated the fact that it wasn't a view of a row of townhouses that it could well have been.

In 2013 I landed on my fucking feet, I bought a dirt cheap repossessed house. It's a double fronted 3 bed end terrace. The back garden is just over 1400 Sq Ft, for a man who spends most of his time away this garden is just the right size. (To any American readers, trust me, for England that's a reasonable sized garden. We don't all live in castles and speak in a posh accent like you've been led to believe!) At the back of this house is a small field and lots of tree's and at the front I have a view of the North York Moors. At the side of the house is a bit of land which is just about big enough for a small extension. The large loft could make a master bedroom. I've got enough space out the back for a large conservatory as well. If I can be arsed to do all that work then by the time my house is finished it will be quite a decent sized pad.

I'm not going to lie to you, it was in a state when I bought it and the gardens are a fucking mess, but this was something I had wanted. Every man needs a project and even if the house had been nice already I still would have gutted it.

When I moved in I was to learn the horrific story of what had happened to the previous occupant. I wouldn't wish it upon anyone. That man's extreme bad luck had directly led to my extreme good luck. Would I change it for this man if I could? The honest answer is probably not. That's just human nature.

In the first year of living there I spent a *lot* of money on it and all I managed to achieve with this money was to get the upstairs finished. In September 2014 all work to the house completely stopped. I had family members telling me to do more of the work myself. But when it comes to painting the exterior of a house or fitting a kitchen, I can tell you that I would rather paper-cut my own foreskin than do that sort of work.

During those horrific winter months of unemployment my house really wasn't the most pleasant place in the world for a man to be living in. Obviously if I hadn't gone to Thailand so many times then the entire house and both gardens could easily have been finished. I don't have any regrets.

The area is I live in is quiet and I still haven't even seen all my neighbours yet, (which suits me down to the ground), but the truth is, it's not where I pictured myself to be living when I was younger. I can say hand on heart that, unless I win the lottery, I'm never going to move from this house and obviously I have my reasons why.

When I was married I had two big goals in life, to be mortgage free aged 50 and thereafter live abroad every winter. Deep down though I knew neither of these goals would be achievable. If my wife and I had stayed together we would've just bought a bigger house and it would've been impossible to pay off the mortgage as early as I would've liked. Also my ex could never have found a job which would enable her to take three or four months off each year. Although I always got my own way when I was married, even I know I wouldn't have been able to disappear each winter on my own.

Now both my goals are very achievable but they will both happen a *lot* sooner than planned. These are no longer goals for my fifties but goals for my forties! Depending on work I *could* be mortgage free aged 40. I know that for my generation that makes me one of the lucky few. As soon as my kids are at colleague age then I'll be joining that list of contractors who jump on a plane abroad in October and don't return again until March. Which, in the scheme of the entire population of our planet, makes me one of the extremely lucky few.

My goals are only possible though because I have thrown away that obsession that nearly every Englishman has…to live in the biggest, nicest house possible. Now that I'm single I can see clearly that, that obsession is pretty pointless and also life destroying. I could go and get mortgaged to the hilt and live in a posh area but what's the fucking point? Houses like that are nothing more than luxury prisons. Debt is stress and the companies who I work for like to take advantage of that stress.

When I was married I always fell straight into the *'employers trap'*! The only time a company will tell its workforce that they've got loads of work is when there is actually loads of *other* work about. The employer is fearful of losing its men so it will dangle a carrot to try and keep them. However in quieter times an employer likes to keep its workforce in a state of perpetual fear! Allowing them to believe that they could lose their job at any moment. When I was the sole breadwinner in a house of four people, I allowed myself to get stressed out by these mind games that companies pull. These days I couldn't give a fuck!

The more debt a person is in, the more stressed out they are and the more miserable they become. I feel like I've had a huge weight lifted off my back and I'll never allow myself to be burdened with that same weight again. There's a quote at the beginning of this book *'Freedom is a myth'*, that quote is true and can *never* be changed. But being debt free and being able to have holidays whenever you feel like it, is as close to 'freedom' as any man is ever going to get.

I'm having my turn on this planet, I'm going to make sure that I enjoy myself. What do I have to thank for this lifestyle that I'm striving for? This trade that I have spent the majority of my working life absolutely hating…I don't hate it anymore.

Of course my long-term goals and plans could quite well be scuppered if a Muslim should ever read this.

CHAPTER NINE

THE NIGGERS OF THE NORTH SEA

Oh how I pity any offshore worker who has been foolish enough to let his wife read this!

1

My trade is what is known as a 'Black Trade'. These are your platers, pipefitters, welders etc. The term 'Black Trade' took on a whole new connotation when I started working offshore though. Whilst I was sat in the heliport waiting to go offshore for the *very* first time, I got talking to a man who had a similar trade to my own. He was going to the same rig as me and when he found out that it was my first time, he did the gentlemanly thing of sitting me on his knee and keeping me right. (Not literally of course) He said to me,

"When you get out there son, you're quickly going to realise that we are the niggers of the North Sea!" It didn't take me long to realise what he meant by that.

The role of a contractor is to jump from job to job. We do the work that is required from us and when it's complete we are given the boot. A job might last one year or it might only last one day. As I write these words at the age of 34 I have worked on more sites/rigs than what I have lived in years.

There is one crucial difference between offshore and onshore life. Working onshore we only ever fraternise with people who have similar jobs to our own, everyone you speak to will also be a contractor who is there for only a limited period of time. When you work offshore you get to mingle with all the long-term staff. As the black trades are only going to be on the rig for a short period of time we are nothing more than a hindrance to the men with permanent positions. We take up their tables in the galley, take up space in their recreational rooms and God forbid that they should ever have to share a room with one of us! We are generally made to feel as welcome as Adolf Hitler at a bar mitzvah. They want us gone as soon as possible!

The worst ones of the lot are the older regulars. From the attitude of these men you'd believe that they had been born on the rig! They completely forget that there was a time when they had been brand new and didn't know their way around the place. They can be so fucking ignorant! Passing through jobs doesn't bother me, not speaking to work colleagues doesn't bother me BUT if I smile at someone or say hello to them then I expect the same response back!

In the scheme of things, working with ignorant men is a very small price to pay for having the offshore lifestyle. I've found that it's a lifestyle that I'm very suited to and it's not just because I love time off. It's because I'm a strange person and there's one thing that I have noticed about all offshore workers, every single one of them is strange. In fact some of these men are *so* strange, they make me seem normal! When you think about it a man *must* have something wrong with his head if he chooses to live on a big rusty skip in the middle of the sea for a good chunk of his year. I don't think all the sea air helps either.

Because of each person's strangeness, it makes socialising slightly more bearable. Workmates aren't your real mates, they're just men that you've been thrown together with, but I've met a handful of men in my short time offshore who I can say that I fully trust. There's a couple of them I would describe as genuine friends. (Don't worry Jamie, you will always be my favourite) But then of course there's the other side of it. There's the men who get on your nerves as well.

There is a long list of names that people could call me, dickhead, wanker, smelly cock...but there is one thing I can never be called and that is a sheep. I have *always* done my own thing in life. Offshore the ratio of sheep is higher than what you find onshore. There are many different ways in which men can behave like sheep and I'm going to discuss two of them. The 'fashion sheep' and what I call the 'verbal sheep'.

We are all guilty of being fashion sheep in one way, I didn't invent or design the clothes that I wear, so ultimately I'm just copying someone else somewhere down the line. But some men seem to act as if they haven't got their own brain! I've noticed two recent fashion trends that have crept in on men a similar age to me, neck tattoos and bushy beards!

A tattoo on the neck to me is a badge. It is a badge which screams out, *'Look at me! I'm a man who suffers from incredibly low self-esteem!'* When I see these men I show them nothing but pity. I never pander to them, I only show them pure, unadulterated pity.

A bushy beard is nothing more than a veil of shame, when I see a man walking around with a mat of pubes on his face it tells me that the man wearing it has completely lost all grip on reality. If you ever see a man wearing both a 'veil of shame' and a badge of 'low self-esteem' my advice to you is to completely ignore every single word that they say to you. They are nothing more than a lost cause…when I look at them I could almost weep!

The worst type of sheep are the verbal sheep. These are the men who say things that they don't mean because they believe it's what the people around them want to hear. There is one problem with this though, if you sit in a room full of men it's impossible to agree with everyone there. The more these verbal sheep try to agree with everyone then the quicker they are caught out. After they've been caught out, nothing else they say will ever be taken seriously.

The two main topics of conversation offshore are how much men hate their wives and how much they hate the food. I would imagine that some men do have genuine reasons to complain about their wives and also there will be men who genuinely dislike the food. But I often wonder how many men are complaining about these two things purely because it's something they think they're supposed to do?

How many men have sat and really enjoyed an offshore meal, practically licked the plate clean and then at the end of it blurted out,

"Urghh! What a disgusting pile of shit! I wouldn't give that to a dog!"

I can remember once working with a man who complained about every single meal that he had, I suspect that he genuinely was a fussy eater. But one time he only ate a third of what was on his plate and he then stood up and loudly said,

"I can't finish that! That's the first time in 15 years of working offshore that I've thrown a plate of food away!"

My immediate thought to myself was, *'That's definitely not the first time that you've done that and it's definitely not the first time that you've said it either.'*

I really don't understand why men feel the need to try and please everyone around them. What's wrong with not being liked by some people? It's fucking normal!

Whilst I'm slagging off my fellow co-workers (and probably many of you reading this book right now) I feel the need to give the divers a special mention. Divers are the most handsome, most humble and unquestionably the most important men in the North Sea. Obviously I'm talking out of my bellend! Divers are the rudest, most arrogant, egotistical wankers in the North Sea! In their job interview arrogance is part of the job description. If the arrogance isn't there then don't worry, it will grow with time. They strut around rigs, not making way in the corridors and not holding doors open for people. They expect everyone else to drop to their knees and start grovelling at their feet!

On one rig I worked on an old chap had just landed and made his way to his room. When he walked in he had the pleasant surprise of seeing a diver sitting there. The diver didn't introduce himself, he simply said,

"What're you doing in here?"

"This is my room."

The diver then said,

"Well this is no good! You'll have to get a room change."

Luckily this old chap was a good old fashioned Scotsman who didn't mince his words,

"Well I've been on this rig for 10 years, so you can fucking change rooms!"

This is just one of many typical diver stories that you will hear.

The worst thing about them is their 'crack'. What a bunch of humourless spastics they all are! I once had the misfortune of sitting in a room full of them and I have never cringed so much in my entire life! They were sat belly laughing at their own pathetic attempts at humour. It was extremely embarrassing and even the ten year old version of myself wouldn't have laughed at what they were saying. I could feel them glancing at me, checking for a reaction and probably thinking that there was something wrong with me for not joining in the merriment! And then worst of all some of them tried to get me involved in their ridiculous conversation! Why can't people just fucking leave me alone?!

Dear reader, please don't ever think that I'm one of those blokes who sits in a room full of people talking about myself because I'm not! I can quite happily sit in a room being ignored by everyone. If there's one thing I like about working with Sweaty Socks it's their ability to sit quietly, wallowing in their own self misery. I'm exactly the same! I can remember having a good conversation with a Scottish colleague one day and he said to me,

"People on here call you miserable, but I don't think that you are."

I replied,

"That's because you're Scottish."

He thought about it for a second and said,

"You're probably right."

2

I got the call to go back offshore in august after another arse-nipping spell of unemployment. I can tell you that it's very disheartening to be in the middle of the supposed busy season and every company you ring tells you that they're paying people off!

My journey started as always in Darlington train station where I will begin my long rail commute. When I boarded the train I had the misfortune of seeing one those disgustingly posh middleclass families. You know the type, incredibly boring and give the rest of us English a bad name. There was a mother, a father and two young daughters. As I walked past one of the girls was just finishing a sentence, I didn't hear what she'd said but I heard her father's reply clearly,

"Yes but that's a double negative"

The girl couldn't have been any older than six! I felt like spewing into my mouth and swallowing it back down again! I suppose people like that aren't as offensive as some of the types you see on that train. Mainly the loud drunken offshore arseholes who have no objection to swearing in front of little children!

I'd purposely got on an early train so that I didn't have a problem getting a seat. This journey can be horrendous at certain times of the day. The rail companies have a tendency to completely oversell the tickets and people can be herded onto the trains like cattle, being forced to stand in the isles and in between carriages! I once overheard one man call it the 'Bangladeshi Express'. Once I sat down I put my iPod on and listened to Wasted Hours by Arcade Fire.

The Eastcoast Mainline is a line of two emotions, northbound deep misery and southbound deep joy. I didn't feel the misery this time, I was just happy to be back in that industry. Sometimes you can make this same journey when you aren't actually going offshore but instead heading to Aberdeen to complete the usual monotonous courses that you have to do before most rig's you go on. There is only one good thing about doing these courses, you get to sample Aberdeen's highbrow culture…or should I say the cities many strip clubs!

The most famous of them all is called Bugsy's and I've never really understood why this is so. Admittedly when the place is full the atmosphere can be lively and fun, *but* there is no such thing as a private dance in this place. When a man does decide that he can no longer resist the allure of staring at a woman's gaping axe-wound, then he'll find himself being dragged to the front of a small stage area, where he is forced to sit facing everyone in the club. When I watch these 'private' dances I'm never looking at the naked woman, I'm looking at the face of the man who is receiving the dance. There are only two types of face that a man will pull when he's put in this position. One is a look of embarrassment and awkwardness with maybe a little giggle to try and hide the fact. The other is a look of pure perversion! These men forget that a whole club full of people are watching them and they will creepily stare at the girl, almost looking like a serial killer getting ready to pounce!

I can remember sitting in there with a mate one time and I said to him,

"Any man who gets a dance in this place has got no self-respect!"

He just nodded. Literally five minutes later I went to the bar to get a round in and when I returned to the table he was gone. I looked at the stage area and there he was getting a dance, staring at the naked woman with beady little eyes!

Of course another wonderful thing about Aberdeen are the many prostitutes and outright slags who reside in the city. A word of warning, sometimes getting one of these women back to your hotel can be a bit of nightmare! The ultra-prudish, draconian Scottish staff don't take kindly to it.

People can say what they like about Aberdoom…yes its grey, yes it's cold and bleak, but it's also incredibly seedy. I love the place!

When I was eventually sat on the chopper, it was a beautiful sunny day. It really is appalling at how much money runs our lives because whenever I'm sat in a chopper in weather like this I'm always having the same thought. *'I hope we have a controlled ditch'*. The reason I'm thinking this is purely because of the lump sum of money that would be paid to me if it did happen. These are thoughts that I keep to myself and for all I know I might be the only man in the North Sea who is having them…but I'm willing to bet that I'm not! Is it normal for a man to be hoping for the helicopter he is sitting on to have technical problems, just so he can get a pay out? I think it's pretty fucking pathetic but that's the power of money for you. How many of you would be willing to have a finger chopped off for a million pounds? (If anyone reading this has been affected by a helicopter ditching, I promise that I mean no offence with that last paragraph. If I have caused offence then I genuinely am sorry.)

When I got on the rig I had the pleasure of seeing my first North Sea sunset in a long time. When I watch them I'm always thinking of Thailand. I don't do myself any favours do I?

Fishermen say that they feel more at home when they're out at sea rather than on land. Since working offshore I can now sort of understand that mentality. When you're surrounded by all that sea Great Britain might as well be on the other side of the world. You are completely detached from everything going on in your homeland. I would imagine that feeling of detachment is also a feeling of freedom to fishermen. Unfortunately for rig workers freedom is the last emotion we're feeling when we're out there.

There are some aspects of offshore life that I hate! When I first started in this industry my impression of the workers was that many of them were cowards...but it didn't take me long to discover the reason why.

The first two rigs I worked on the jobs went smoothly and I received good assessments from both platforms. The third rig I worked on was a decommissioning job and I was told at the start that I would get a minimum of one year. I only lasted 2 trips! I have worked in some dangerous shitholes in my time and this job was easily the second most dangerous place I have worked in. It wasn't what I would ever have expected to see in the North Sea.

During my second trip a man suffered quite a serious injury and unfortunately for him he wasn't the first. I felt compelled to have a *very* frank conversation with both the Safety Officer and my manager. Needless to say, my relationship with both of these men was very *frosty* for the remainder of the trip. When I got home I was introduced to the offshore NRB culture. NRB means 'Not Required Back'. If you so much as look at a manager in the wrong way he can send your company an very simple email, Joe Bloggs NRB. That's your employment on that particular rig terminated with no explanation needed. It's an absolute scandal! When I was NRB'd the hardest thing for me to accept was the fact that in-between my two trips and during my *own* time off I had been forced to endure an eight hour Health & Safety seminar! Hypocritical isn't a strong enough word!

Another thing I hate is the 'safety card culture'. Safety cards are used to record both good and bad aspects of a rigs safety and this information is used to create data. This data lets them see what they're doing right and what needs improving on. However many rigs take it too far. They make the cards compulsory, telling every single person that they have to fill in at least one card per shift. The backstabbing becomes even worse than what is found in the Houses of Parliament. This creates an atmosphere of poison and mistrust! I don't know of any workplace which benefits from an atmosphere like that.

Also it's a completely pointless exercise as it is usual to see men grab 14 cards on their first shift and fill them all out with lies. The cards will then be placed in their lockers ready to hand in at the end of every shift. The safety departments on these rigs are creating data based on complete falsehoods. It's an absolute waste of money! Money that could be used to increase our wages.

Don't even get me started on the draconian Health & Safety signs filling every spare inch of wall space! On one rig there was even a mirror with a sign on the top of it! It read, 'This Person Is Responsible For Your Safety'. I thought to myself, *'I can't even look in a fucking mirror without the cunts telling me what to do!'*

My new job turned out to be only for one trip. If I'm really lucky I might get two or three more trips this year. The industry is in complete turmoil at this moment in time and cuts are being made across the board. One cost cutting exercise is imposing a new horrific shift pattern onto the regular hands. The general consensus is that none of these cutbacks will be reversed when the industry stabilises again.

As usual it's the black trades who suffer the most. Projects have been shelved and some completely scrapped. It makes you wonder what these companies do with their huge profits. Common sense would dictate that this is the perfect time to invest, so when the oil prices do inevitably rise again the rigs can run at full capacity. Unfortunately every business in the world seems to be short sighted and only seem to care about the profits of the day and not about the people who actually make them all their money.

Don't worry too much about us black trade's though dear reader, you'll be pleased to hear there will still be plenty of European tradesmen having a carefree winter working in the British sectors of the North Sea! It's just *fucking* WRONG!

If you are on a rig now reading this in your bunk bed, I might just be the man laid in the opposite bunk. Waiting for you to fall asleep... so that I can have a danger wank!

CHAPTER TEN

THE TRIALS AND TRIBULATIONS OF A SELF-PUBLISHED BASTARD

Trying to sell a book is a bit like leaving your front door...you might have a pleasant walk or you might just end up stepping into a big pile of smelly dogshit!

I had no expectations whatsoever for my debut, but I still felt disappointed that I hadn't been able to advertise it in the way I had planned. I'll admit that I don't have the technical knowhow nor the drive to do any real advertising for my books. I'll certainly never spend money on advertising them. I know there are many self-published authors who spend thousands on their books!

I pay a publisher a relatively small fee to format my books, do some other tedious things that I won't bore you with and then put them on sale. I could quite easily learn how to do these things myself but I really can't be bothered to. The way I see it, everyone who has a hobby spends money on it. But after that fee I'm not willing to pay for anything else, it takes nearly 100 sales just to make my money back.

After the initial setback of trying to advertise Thailand After Divorce it did start to sell in dribs and drabs. Three and a half months later on Monday 19th January 2015 my second book Rigs, Pigs & Dirty Digs was released to the world and I must admit that I had higher expectations for that one. It wasn't released until very late in the day and as soon as it was I placed an advert on three Facebook forums. I only had any joy with one of those posts and I have to give a huge thanks here to Daniel Lawson at The North Sea Tigers. That man read my post, liked it and put it straight onto the main page. It was that small little action of his that made a big impact on my book sales. His continued help and support means that he has become the backbone of Barry J Steel.

Within two hours of that post going up my second book had equalled the sales of my debut. By the end of the night, after being on sale only a handful of hours, it had more than doubled those sales.

When your average Joe decides that he's going to start writing a book, the idea of anyone actually reading it one day initially seems preposterous. When it's finished and people do start buying it, I can guarantee you that it's a very strange feeling, knowing that complete strangers are reading about your life. And what's even more bizarre is knowing that those strangers have spent their own hard earned money to do so! Even weirder still is knowing that people in a different country are also reading about you! You can imagine my surprise and delight when the day after Rigs was released some Yank had given my book a five star review on Amazon. He goes by the name of JeffKnowsStuff. If you're reading this now Jeff then do not underestimate how happy that review made me. I believe it's also the reason some of your fellow countrymen have carried on buying it.

I want to take this opportunity to thank everyone who has taken the time out to review my books. Even some of the negative ones got a chuckle out of me. And to Gerald, the man who gave Rigs five stars and asked me to keep my next book 'dirty'…I hope I haven't disappointed you.

I noticed that a few days after Rigs was released a new section had appeared on its Amazon page. '*Customers who bought this also bought*' I had to stifle a giggle when I saw The Wolf Of Wall Street on there. I can assure you now that there's absolutely no similarities at all between myself and the character in that book! (Unfortunately for me).

Amazon has its own book charts and for some reason they kept placing my book in inappropriate categories. My book went to the number one spot in the incredibly popular 'Mining and Geology' chart and it also peaked at number five in the 'Engineering Biography' chart. Anyone buying that book purely because of its position in those charts would've been in for a bit of a shock!

My biggest delight was when people started to buy Thailand off the back of Rigs. Having your own books is a bit like having children, it's impossible not to have a favourite. My debut book is my favourite of the two and although the sales figures show that you disagree with me, it was with that first book where I actually had a story to tell. The second book was just an excuse for me to carry on writing. The three proudest days of my life so far…the birth of my two kids and the day Thailand After Divorce came through the letterbox.

In February 2015 I received my first royalty cheque. It only covered the first couple of month's paperback sales for Thailand. It was a paltry sum and I didn't bother cashing it, instead I had it framed.

I'm going to take the risk of completely boring you now by taking you through the writing process. I'll keep it brief.

Writing is the easy bit for me, my books are nothing more than diaries and *anyone* can write a diary. (That makes YOU quite a voyeuristic person, paying to read someone else's diary…nosey bastard!) The hard part for me is the editing and proof reading.

Once the book is finished you have to decide what to leave in and what to take out. What might interest me, might be completely boring to someone else. When I read my first book back to myself I realised that the title could've been changed to 'Ego After Divorce'. Although those stories were very good memories for me, I knew that people reading them would've just thought that I was a bit of a dick, so I cut loads out of that book. When I read Rigs back I took out a couple of stories where I feared people reading them might have believed them to be falsehoods.

When I've read this book back I've realised that it's entirely about my 'dark side' and someone reading it could quite easily believe that I don't have any redeeming qualities whatsoever. Although I haven't really cut anything out, I have gone back over it and toned it down quite a bit. I'll admit that I don't like the first chapter of this book at all, but I knew if I didn't write it then the ending of my debut would just seem like complete nonsense.

The proof reading stage is a bit of a fucking nightmare! Because I'm the one who has written them, when I read my books back to myself, I don't necessarily read the words on the page, but rather what I think it should say in my own head. That's why my books are littered with mistakes, but hopefully this is something that I'm getting bittar attt. Once again this comes down to me being a bit of a mingebag and not wanting to pay someone else to do it for me.

I know that in my industry there are thousands of creative men who feel like they have been wasted in life. Some men are brilliant artists, some are musicians and some are even aspiring filmmakers (watch the 'Subsea 7 Africa' video on YouTube). I know there will be lots of you who have toyed with the idea of writing a book at least once in your life and I know that many of you will be able to produce far superior work to my efforts. I urge you to pick up your pens and give it a go. You don't have to worry about *will it be published?* because *anyone* can publish a book these days with self-publishing. Even if nobody wanted to buy it, it's still a good feeling when you see it on your own bookcase at home. Don't start it because you think it will make you money, start it because it's something that you really want to do. It's one of the most enjoyable hobbies that you could ever have. And remember one important thing dear reader. If people with absolutely no worth in society, such as thick thug scum and pointless

167

celebrities, can write about themselves, then so can you!

A couple of men have told me that when they read Rigs, they felt like they were reading about themselves and that's the whole point of it I suppose. Although we men all have our own different personalities, our lives and experiences are remarkably similar. When we're kids we play out, in our early teens we sample naughty things, in our later teens we spend hours in cars pointlessly driving around and then apparently we become men. When we're young we believe that becoming a man is something that is going to happen overnight on one of our birthdays. We spend years being told by society that we are men without actually feeling like one. It's a *very* long process. As adults we all hate working for someone else, we hate paying bills, there's always at least one problem happening in our lives at any one time and at some point we have all questioned what our role in the world is supposed to be. So what do we do to escape the daily grind? We get lost in books, music and films, we get off our faces on drugs and alcohol, we have sex with women and our hands. I'm no different from you…except I'm a bit partial to skull fucking the odd ladyboy.

Whilst writing this book I've noticed a very peculiar trait with us men...we seem to connect to objects more than what we do to people. My favourite author was a socialist painter and decorator and when I read his book I identified a lot with the main character. However I know if I'd ever had the chance to meet the author I probably would've found him to be quite annoying. (His name is Robert Tressell and he's a pretty big influence on this book. That comment will have him spinning in his grave!) It's the same with my favourite lyricist Roger Waters, I love his lyrics but I would never want to be sat in his company.

I know that not everyone who has read this will have enjoyed it, but to those of you who have I'd be willing to place a bet. If you'd spent the last hour sitting with me listening to me tell you some of the stories from this book and listening to my views and opinions, you would probably just think that I was some boring tit, saying things you'd heard a thousand times before. Right now you're sat on your own, enjoying your own space, you've created your own image of me in your head and you feel more connected to the black ink on white paper than what you would to me in real life. We really are a strange species.

Dear reader, please don't read this chapter and believe that I have any sort of moderate success with my books. Keep in mind that I'm a tradesman who has written a couple of daft self-published books and I haven't advertised them properly. A real author would find my sales laughable! BUT, although my sales aren't quite into the thousands just yet, I've still done alright.

After the initial spurt of sales in the first month of Rigs being released, they died down to a steady flow and they have continued to sell from those handful of posts on a Facebook forum. Sales in the UK, US, EU and Australia. I would like to say that I've gone global but that would be a bit of a big fib!

I said at the end of my last book that my hobby won't make me rich. But my hobby has put a nice chunk towards a holiday...

Are you one of these weirdo's who reads the final chapter first? Go back to the start and read it properly you fucking idiot!

CHAPTER ELEVEN

THE MEANING OF IT ALL?

The question *'What is the meaning of life?'* is regarded as *the* unanswerable question. However, to those of us who are secular it is one of the simplest questions, with a very simple answer…

'To survive and reproduce.'

That's all life is, we are born, we survive and one day we all die. It's what we do with our time and what we leave behind that's important. Preservation of genes is a *must*. Most people who live and who *have* lived will only ever leave behind their genes and nothing else.

I am grateful to my great, great grandparents for allowing me to exist. Do I care about these people? How can I truly care about people who I have never met and whom I know nothing about? It would've been the same for them when asked about the long line of offspring that would appear from their genes.

I have been told that the digital versions of my books will last as long as the remaining lifespan of the human race. It's a strange thought for me that *possibly* one hundred years after I have died my great, great grandkids could one day be sat reading my books. Would they be ashamed? Would they be amused? One thing is for definite, they would know a *lot* more about their great, great granddad than I do about my own.

Are this future offspring of mine sat reading this book right now and looking back to this age that I lived in? Laughing about our primitive technology and medicine? Are they sat in disbelief that people living in England used to believe in God? Are they astounded that each household in England could have as many kids or cars as they wanted? Will they be able to understand this version of English that we used to speak? Will this symbol '£' mean anything to them? Will they be confused that our skin used to wrinkle as we got older? Are they dumbfounded that men used to use their hands to masturbate? Will they always laugh about that group of fame hungry idiots who volunteered for the mission to Mars, knowing they could never return home and the tragedy that unfolded on that flight as they realised their deaths were imminent? Will they disbelieve that the USA and UK used to unashamedly suck up to that desolate, arid shithole formerly known as Saudi Arabia? Can they imagine a planet that wasn't ran by China? And the biggest question of all that I have for this future offspring of mine? I wonder… did any of you turn out to be like me?

THE END

ALL PROCEEDS FROM THIS BOOK
ARE DONATED TO THE
B.J.STEEL WITNESS RELOCATION
PROGRAM

Lightning Source UK Ltd.
Milton Keynes UK
UKOW06f1947311017

311970UK00013B/1030/P